CAKE DECORATING

step by step

GIOVANNA TORRICO

PHOTOGRAPHY DEIRDRE ROONEY

CAKE DECORATING

step by step

*Simple instructions for gorgeous cakes,
cupcakes and cookies*

MURDOCH BOOKS

SYDNEY · LONDON

CONTENTS

Introduction

After I became a mother, I started using my own mother's age-old recipes to make my children's birthday cakes. Each year I made them more and more elaborate and friends started asking me to make cakes for them, too. As I enjoyed creating new designs I realised that baking was where my passion lay. I hope that this book will birth, or help develop, such a passion in you, too! In it I have provided you with all the baking and decorating techniques and tips you need to get creative with your own cakes and cookies.

Everything has been organised to make it easy for both beginners and experienced cake makers alike to master all the methods and recipes.

Throughout the book practical, accessible text is accompanied by clear photography so that you are able to follow all the techniques closely as you try them out for yourself.

The book starts with the preparation and planning of a cake – from the list of the tools you need to the way to line a cake tin. The basic cake and cookie recipes are then described, followed by recipes for covering and filling them.

In layering, covering and stacking you will learn how to get the perfect cake ready for all the decorations you may wish to include. The next chapters then explain the following decorating techniques and methods in detail: hand piping, hand moulding and the use of different cutters and silicone moulds.

The book ends with some of my favourite cake and cookie projects, which amalgamate much of the expertise you will have perfected by this point into specific designs. These are totally interchangeable so feel free to experiment and create your own cakes, simply using the designs as inspiration for your own imagination.

Enjoy!

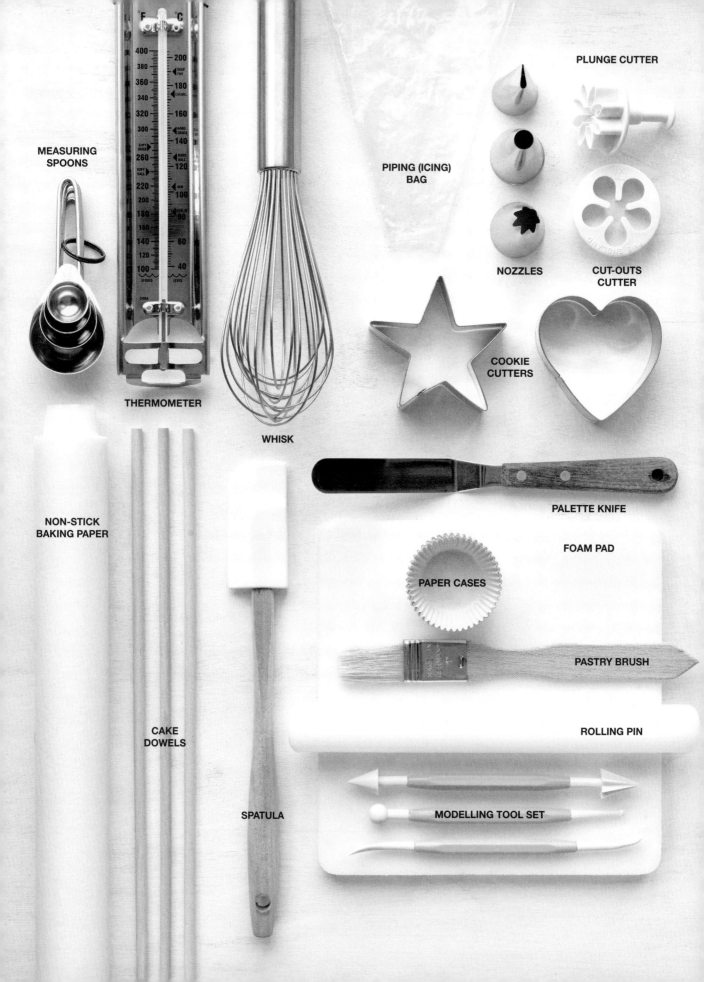

MEASURING
SPOONS

THERMOMETER

WHISK

PIPING (ICING)
BAG

PLUNGE CUTTER

NOZZLES

CUT-OUTS
CUTTER

COOKIE
CUTTERS

NON-STICK
BAKING PAPER

PALETTE KNIFE

FOAM PAD

PAPER CASES

PASTRY BRUSH

CAKE
DOWELS

ROLLING PIN

SPATULA

MODELLING TOOL SET

Tools & Equipment

Before you begin baking, ensure you have all the tools and equipment that you'll need on hand. Here is a summary of the things needed for baking and decorating cakes and cookies.

BAKING TRAY: a rimless, flat, metal sheet, designed for baking rows of cookies.

CAKE BOARDS: of various sizes and thicknesses.

CAKE DOWELS: use to create a strong internal support system for tiered cakes.

CAKE STANDS AND PLATES: many pretty, stylish stands and plates are available.

CAKE TINS: traditional shapes are round, square and rectangular.

COOKIE CUTTERS: use to cut decorative shapes from rolled-out dough.

CUPCAKE TINS: metal baking tins with usually 6 or 12 cups used to bake muffins and cupcakes.

FOAM PAD: useful for working on to add veins to flowers and leaves, for softening the edges of flower petals and for frilling.

FREESTANDING OR STANDMIXER: takes all the effort out of beating cake mixtures or mixing frosting ingredients together.

GRATER: use to remove the zest from citrus fruit or to grate chocolate.

MEASURING SPOONS: use for measuring small amounts of ingredients like natural vanilla extract, salt or baking powder.

METAL SPOONS: have many uses in the kitchen.

MIXING BOWLS: at least one or two large and small bowls are a must.

MODELLING TOOL SET: a starter kit has a variety of ball tools, a scallop tool, a tool with a cone at the end, a veining tool and a dog bone tool.

NON-STICK BAKING PAPER: use to line baking trays and cake tins, and for folding into paper cones to create piping (icing) bags.

PAPER CASES: cupcake liners are convenient, save on cleaning and are very easy to use.

PASTRY BRUSHES: use to spread glazes and egg wash, to grease tins or to brush excess flour and icing (confectioners') sugar from dough and sugarpaste (fondant).

PIPING (ICING) BAGS AND NOZZLES: use for cake and cookie decorating; piping bags can also be fitted with decorative nozzles for piping frosting and cream.

PIZZA CUTTER: handy for trimming excess rolled sugarpaste (fondant) after covering cakes or cutting strips of sugarpaste.

PLUNGER CUTTERS: use to add details to your cake, cupcakes and cookies.

ROLLING PINS: useful for rolling sugarpaste (fondant), pastry and cookie doughs.

SIEVE: use to sift and eliminate or separate clumps from flour, cocoa powder and icing (confectioners') sugar.

SILICONE MOULDS: easy to use, flexible and highly detailed moulds.

SPATULAS: these have many uses including scraping batters from the sides and bottoms of bowls, as well as spreading, filling, folding and stirring.

SUGARPASTE (FONDANT) SMOOTHER: ingenious tool that gives a sugarpaste-covered cake a satiny, smooth even finish.

THERMOMETER: useful for Italian meringue or when mixing butter into chocolate ganache.

WHISKS: use to whisk dry ingredients together, beat eggs or whip cream.

WIRE RACKS: use to cool cakes after baking. Also useful to place a cake on when pouring a ganache over it.

WOODEN SPOONS: use for beating cake mixtures and frostings.

NATURAL VANILLA EXTRACT

COLOURED SUGARPASTE (FONDANT)

VANILLA BEANS

CHOCOLATE: (CLOCKWISE FROM TOP) MILK, DARK AND WHITE

RAW (DEMERARA) SUGAR

CASTER (SUPERFINE) SUGAR

LIGHT BROWN SUGAR

WALNUTS

POLENTA (CORNMEAL)

GLUCOSE SYRUP

ICING (CONFECTIONERS') SUGAR

POWDERED FOOD COLOURS

GLYCERINE

COCOA POWDER

Ingredients

Have a good supply of the following essential ingredients in your kitchen when baking and decorating cakes.

EGGS

These play an important role in the baking world, adding structure, colour and flavour. It is the balance between eggs and flour that helps to provide the height and texture to cakes.

DAIRY PRODUCTS

One of the most widely used categories in baking ingredients is the dairy products. These include butter, milk, yoghurt, thick (double) cream and mascarpone.

WHEAT

Wheat-based flour is made by grinding wheat – the most popular grain used in baking – and includes plain (all-purpose) flour and self-raising flour.

POLENTA

Made from ground cornmeal, polenta has a rich yellow colour and adds a lovely flavour.

SWEETENERS

A large variety of sugars can be produced by extracting and purifying sugar from sugar cane, including caster (superfine) sugar, light brown sugar, raw (demerara) sugar, icing (confectioners') sugar and glucose syrup.

FOOD COLOURS

These come in many forms, such as liquid, powder, paste or gel. The most reliable is the gel because it is more concentrated so will not affect the final results when it is added to a recipe (for example into buttercream). Also, the result will be much brighter and more saturated than the liquid form. (Powdered colours can also come in a sparkly range, as shown at left.)

PIPING GEL

This is a sweet gel that can be used in many different ways in cake decorating, such as glazing sugarpaste (fondant). It can also be added to buttercream to give elasticity when applying writing to the surface of a cake.

LEAVENING AGENT

Baking powder contributes in numerous ways to baking – not only does it leaven certain ingredients (reacting with the liquid to cause the cake to rise), it also tenderises, adds flavour and provides a finer crumb.

THICKENING AGENT

The simplest way to thicken food is to add an ingredient that is itself thickened, such as egg, cream or yoghurt. When this is not possible, a thickening agent can be added, such as powdered gelatine. Its function is to absorb a large quantity of liquid.

SOFTENING AGENT

Glycerine is a softening agent in the form of a clear, odourless syrup. It has the property to attract moisture and is used in baking to help cakes stay moist.

FLAVOURINGS

Chocolate (dark, milk and white), cocoa powder, vanilla (beans and extract), almond extract, coffee, salt and white wine vinegar are all flavourings used in cakes and cookies.

CULINARY NUTS

These are dry, edible fruits or seeds usually with a high fat content and they are used in a wide variety of roles within baking. Some examples include walnuts, almond meal and pistachios.

POPPY SEEDS

This is an oilseed harvested from the opium poppy (the tiny, edible black seeds are found in the heads). They have a slightly nutty aroma and taste and are widely used in baking.

FRUITS

Various fruits are used to add flavour and decoration to cakes, such as lemons, oranges, blueberries and strawberries.

Lining a Round Tin

1/// Place the tin on top of a sheet of non-stick baking paper, draw a circle round it and cut out the shape with scissors.

2/// Lightly grease the inside of the tin. Cut a strip of baking paper long enough to cover the tin's circumference exactly and the height plus an additional 1 cm (½ in) to overhang. Fold over the extra 1 cm (½ in) along the long edge.

3/// Use scissors to snip diagonal cuts at 2.5 cm (1 in) intervals along the folded part of the strip of baking paper.

4/// Line the inside of the tin, placing the strip around the edge with the snipped part sitting down onto the lightly greased base of the tin. Place the circular piece of baking paper on the base of the tin.

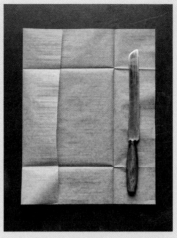

1/// Place the tin on top of a sheet of non-stick baking paper, and fold the paper up on the left, right, front and back sides of the tin.

2/// Crease the baking paper and cut to size. In this way, the baking paper should be big enough to cover the base and sides all-in-one.

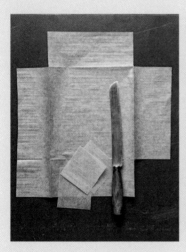

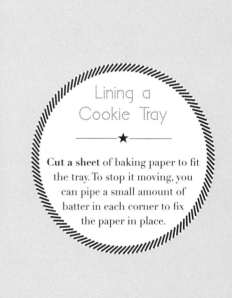

Lining a Cookie Tray

★

Cut a sheet of baking paper to fit the tray. To stop it moving, you can pipe a small amount of batter in each corner to fix the paper in place.

3/// Fold the two side pieces in, then cut partway up the fold (the cut section should make a square or rectangle). Repeat this process on both ends of both sides.

4/// Place the paper into the tin and fold in the corners. Once it fits well, remove the paper, grease the inside of the tin, then place the paper back. This method ensures that there are no gaps in the lining.

Making a Paper Piping Bag

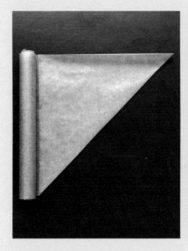

1/// Make a square from a sheet of non-stick baking paper and fold it diagonally across to create 2 triangles.

2/// Place the long side away from you and the opposite point facing you, then curl the right side and bring it in to meet the point.

3/// Lift the cone up, holding the 2 points that now meet in the centre. Wrap the left corner all the way around the cone to meet the other 2 points, so that they line up together. Gently tease the base until you have a sharp pointed tip at the end of the bag.

4/// Fold the points of the bag down into itself, tear 1 notch and fold it down to seal and secure the bag.

Filling a Disposable Piping Bag

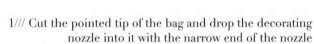

1/// Cut the pointed tip of the bag and drop the decorating nozzle into it with the narrow end of the nozzle pointing downwards.

2/// Fold down the open end over your hand to form a cuff.

3/// Fill the bag about half full, unfold the cuff and twist the bag as close to the mixture as possible.

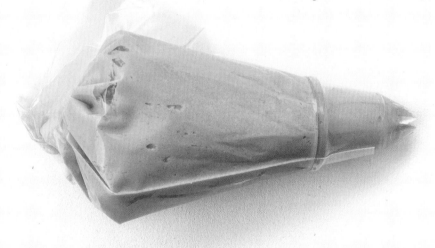

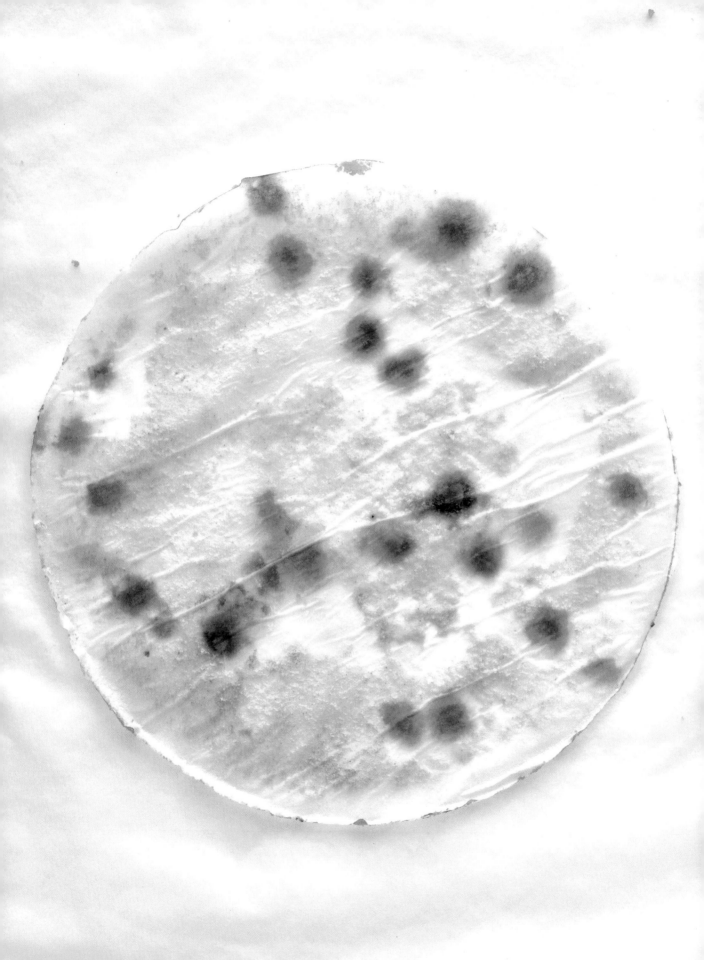

chapter

1

BASIC CAKE
& COOKIE
RECIPES

Vanilla Sponge Cake

MAKES: 18 CM (7 IN) ROUND CAKE   SERVES: 8–10
PREPARATION TIME: 30 MINUTES   COOKING TIME: 45 MINUTES
COOLING TIME: 30 MINUTES

225 g (8 oz/1½ cups) self-raising flour
85 g (3 oz) plain (all-purpose) flour
2 teaspoons baking powder
225 g (8 oz) unsalted butter, softened
225 g (8 oz/1 cup) caster (superfine) sugar
*2 vanilla beans, split in half lengthways
and seeds scraped out*
4 large eggs, lightly beaten

3 tablespoons full-cream (whole) milk
100 g (3½ oz) plain yoghurt

For the vanilla syrup
50 g (1¾ oz) caster (superfine) sugar
2 teaspoons natural vanilla extract

Preheat the oven to 170°C (325°F) and line one 18 cm (7 in) round springform cake tin with non-stick baking paper.

Sift the flours and baking powder together into a bowl and set aside.

To make the vanilla syrup, gently heat 100 ml (3½ fl oz) water, the sugar and vanilla in a small saucepan over low heat, stirring, for 2 minutes until the sugar has dissolved. Remove from the heat and set aside.

For the cake, using a standmixer, cream the butter, sugar and just the seeds from the vanilla beans in a mixing bowl for 5 minutes, or until light and fluffy. Add the beaten eggs, a little at a time, to the creamed butter mixture, still beating to prevent the mixture curdling. If it does separate just add a teaspoonful of flour and continue beating, occasionally scraping down the bowl with a spatula.

Add the sifted dry ingredients to the batter, followed by the milk. Beat in the yoghurt. Pour the cake mixture into the prepared cake tin, creating a well in the centre to prevent a large hump from rising. Bake the cake for about 45 minutes (check it after 30 minutes), or until the cake is springy to the touch and a skewer inserted into the middle comes out clean.

Remove the cake from the oven and leave it to cool in the tin for 10 minutes before turning it out onto a wire rack. Peel off the lining paper and using a skewer poke some holes all over the cake, making sure that the skewer goes through to the bottom. Drizzle or brush the cake with the vanilla syrup and leave it to cool completely.

You can store the cake wrapped in plastic wrap for 3 days or in the freezer for up to a month. Defrost overnight.

Chocolate Truffle Cake

MAKES: 18 CM (7 IN) ROUND CAKE   SERVES: 8–10
PREPARATION TIME: 30 MINUTES   COOKING TIME: 45 MINUTES
COOLING TIME: 30 MINUTES

200 g (7 oz/1⅓ cups) plain (all-purpose) flour
200 g (7 oz) dark chocolate (at least
70% cocoa), broken into pieces
250 g (9 oz) unsalted butter, softened

325 g (11½ oz) soft light brown sugar
1 teaspoon natural vanilla extract
5 large eggs, lightly beaten

Preheat the oven to 170°C (325°F) and line two 18 cm (7 in) round springform cake tins with non-stick baking paper.

Sift the flour into a bowl and set aside.

Put the chocolate into a heatproof bowl, set over but not touching a saucepan of gently simmering water (known as a bain-marie) and leave until melted, which will take about 5 minutes. Once melted, take the bowl off the pan and leave to cool for 5 minutes.

Using a standmixer, cream the butter, sugar and vanilla together for 5 minutes, or until light and fluffy. Add the beaten eggs, a little at a time, mixing well after each addition. While beating, pour the chocolate into the mixture in a steady stream. Add the sifted flour to the mixture and mix it in slowly.

Spoon the mixture evenly into the prepared tins and bake for 45 minutes (check them after 30 minutes), or until the cakes are springy to the touch and a skewer inserted into the middle comes out clean. The cakes should be well risen with a crust.

Remove the cakes from the oven and leave to cool completely in the tins before turning out onto a wire rack and peeling off the lining papers. The crust will sink back into the cakes as they cool.

You can store the cakes wrapped in plastic wrap for 3 days or in the freezer for up to a month. Defrost overnight.

Ombre Cake

MAKES: 18 CM (7 IN) ROUND CAKE   SERVES: 8–10
PREPARATION TIME: 45 MINUTES
COOKING TIME: 15–20 MINUTES EACH
COOLING TIME: 30 MINUTES

325 g (11½ oz) self-raising flour
325 g (11½ oz) unsalted butter, softened
325 g (11½ oz) caster (superfine) sugar
2 teaspoons natural vanilla extract
5 large eggs, lightly beaten
5 liquid food colours of your choice

Preheat the oven to 170°C (325°F) and line five 18 cm (7 in) round springform cake tins with non-stick baking paper. Sift the flour into a bowl and set aside.

Using a standmixer, cream the butter, sugar and vanilla for 5 minutes, or until light and fluffy. Add the beaten eggs, a little at a time, still beating to prevent the mixture curdling. If it does separate, just add a teaspoonful of flour and continue beating, occasionally scraping down the side of the bowl with a spatula.

Fold in the sifted flour with a spatula, and divide the mixture into five small bowls. Using a clean spatula for each, stir in a different food colour to each of the bowls. Add the colour a little at a time until you reach the desired shade and make sure that the colour is thoroughly mixed into the cake mixture.

Pour the cake mixture into the prepared tins and bake for 15–20 minutes, or until the cakes are springy to the touch and a skewer inserted into the middle comes out clean.

Remove the cakes from the oven and leave to cool in the tins for 10 minutes. Then turn them out onto wire racks, peel off the lining papers and leave to cool completely.

You can store the cakes wrapped in plastic wrap for 3 days or in the freezer for up to a month. Defrost overnight.

Lemon & Poppy Seed Drizzle Cake

MAKES: 18 CM (17 IN) ROUND CAKE   SERVES: 8–10
PREPARATION TIME: 30 MINUTES   COOKING TIME: 35–40 MINUTES
COOLING TIME: 30 MINUTES

210 g (7½ oz) self-raising flour
2 teaspoons baking powder
170 g (6 oz) caster (superfine) sugar
finely grated zest and juice of 2 lemons
170 g (6 oz) unsalted butter, softened
3 eggs, lightly beaten
1½ tablespoons poppy seeds

For the lemon syrup
100 g (3½ oz) caster (superfine) sugar
finely grated zest of 2 lemons
100 ml (3½ fl oz) lemon juice

Preheat the oven to 180°C (350°F) and line one 18 cm (7 in) round springform cake tin with non-stick baking paper. Sift the flour and baking powder together into a bowl and set aside.

For the syrup, gently heat the sugar, lemon zest and juice in a saucepan over low heat, stirring, for 2 minutes, or until the sugar has dissolved. Remove from the heat and set aside.

Put the cake ingredients, including the sifted flour mixture, into a bowl and beat with a standmixer for 5–8 minutes. Pour into the tin and bake for 35–40 minutes, or until the cake is springy to the touch and a skewer inserted into the middle comes out clean.

Remove the cake from the oven and leave to cool in the tin for 5 minutes. Then, turn it out onto a wire rack and peel off the lining paper.

While the cake is still warm, use a skewer to poke some holes all over it, going right to the bottom. (Uncooked spaghetti can be used as an alternative to a skewer for this.) Drizzle the lemon syrup over the top and leave it to cool completely.

You can store the cake wrapped in plastic wrap for 3 days or in the freezer for up to a month. Defrost overnight.

Coffee & Walnut Cake

MAKES: 18 CM (7 IN) ROUND CAKE   SERVES: 8–10
PREPARATION TIME: 20 MINUTES   COOKING TIME: 35–40 MINUTES
COOLING TIME: 30 MINUTES

150 g (5½ oz/1 cup) self-raising flour
1½ teaspoons baking powder
75 g (2½ oz) walnut halves
150 g (5½ oz) unsalted butter, softened
150 g (5½ oz/⅔ cup) caster (superfine) sugar
3 large eggs, lightly beaten
2 tablespoons freshly made black coffee

For the coffee syrup
50 g (1¾ oz/¼ cup) raw (demerara) sugar
50 ml (1¾ fl oz) freshly made black coffee

Preheat the oven to 160°C (315°F) and line two 18 cm (7 in) round springform cake tins with non-stick baking paper. Sift the flour and baking powder together into a bowl and set aside.

For the syrup, stir the sugar in the hot coffee until it has dissolved. Set aside.

Spread the walnuts out on a baking tray and toast in the oven for about 7–8 minutes, keeping an eye on them as they can burn easily. Take them out of the oven and chop roughly. Set aside.

Put the butter, sugar, eggs, chopped walnuts and coffee into a bowl, add the sifted dry ingredients and, using a standmixer, whisk for 5 minutes, or until everything is well combined.

Divide the mixture between the prepared tins, level the surfaces and bake for 35–40 minutes, or until the cakes are springy to the touch and a skewer inserted into the middle comes out clean.

Remove the cakes from the oven. Using a skewer, poke some holes all over the top of the cakes, making sure that the skewer goes right to the bottom of the cakes, then brush the syrup all over. Leave the cakes to cool in the tins for 10 minutes. Turn out the cakes onto wire racks, peel off the lining papers and leave the cakes to cool completely.

You can store the cakes wrapped in plastic wrap for 3 days or in the freezer for up to a month. Defrost overnight.

Orange Polenta Cake

MAKES: 20 CM (8 IN) ROUND CAKE   SERVES: 10–12
PREPARATION TIME: 20 MINUTES   COOKING TIME: 45 MINUTES
COOLING TIME: 30 MINUTES

150 g (5½ oz/¾ cup) polenta (cornmeal)
150 g (5½ oz/1½ cups) almond meal
2 teaspoons baking powder
200 g (7 oz) unsalted butter, softened
200 g (7 oz) caster (superfine) sugar
3 large eggs, lightly beaten
finely grated zest and juice of 1 orange

For the orange syrup
100 g (3½ oz) caster (superfine) sugar
juice of 1 orange

Preheat the oven to 180°C (350°F) and line one 20 cm (8 in) round springform cake tin with non-stick baking paper.

For the syrup put the sugar and orange juice in a saucepan and bring to the boil. Reduce the heat and simmer, stirring, for 5 minutes. Set aside to cool.

Sift the polenta, almond meal and baking powder together into a bowl and set aside.

Using a standmixer, cream the butter and sugar together for 5 minutes, or until light and fluffy. Add the beaten eggs, a little at a time, still beating with the mixer to prevent the mixture curdling. Once the mixture is combined, beat in the sifted dry ingredients, then the orange zest and juice until combined.

Pour the mixture into the prepared cake tin, creating a well in the centre to prevent a large hump from rising, and bake for about 45 minutes (check it after 30 minutes), or until the cake is springy to the touch and a skewer inserted into the middle comes out clean.

Remove the cake from the oven and leave to cool in the tin for 10 minutes, then turn it out onto a wire rack and peel off the lining paper. Using a skewer, poke some holes all over the cake, making sure that the skewer goes right to the bottom and leave to cool completely. Once the cake is cool drizzle the orange syrup over the top.

You can store the cake wrapped in plastic wrap for 3 days or in the freezer for up to a month. Defrost overnight.

Red Velvet Cake

MAKES: 18 CM (7 IN) ROUND CAKE   SERVES: 10–12
PREPARATION TIME: 30 MINUTES   COOKING TIME: 25 MINUTES EACH
COOLING TIME: 30 MINUTES

250 ml (9 fl oz/1 cup) buttermilk
450 g (1 lb/ 3 cups) plain (all-purpose) flour
30 g (1 oz/¼ cup) cocoa powder
1 teaspoon salt
2 teaspoons baking powder
185 g (6½ oz) unsalted butter, softened
450 g (1 lb/2 cups) caster (superfine) sugar
1 teaspoon natural vanilla extract

3 large eggs, lightly beaten
2 teaspoons red food paste colour
1 tablespoon white wine vinegar

Preheat the oven to 170°C (325°F) and line four 18 cm (7 in) round springform cake tins with non-stick baking paper.

If you can't find buttermilk, you can make your own by adding 2 teaspoons of lemon juice to 240 ml (8 fl oz) of milk. Leave this to rest for 5–10 minutes before using.

Sift the flour, cocoa powder, salt and baking powder together into a bowl and set aside. Using a standmixer, cream the butter, sugar and vanilla together for 5–10 minutes, or until light and fluffy.

Add the beaten eggs, a small amount at a time, still beating with the mixer to prevent the mixture from curdling.

Stir the red food colour into the buttermilk. Alternating, add some of the buttermilk and

then some of the sifted dry ingredients to the butter mixture, until all added. Finally, add the vinegar but don't overmix.

Pour the cake mixture into the prepared cake tins and create a well in the centre of each to prevent a large hump from rising. Bake for about 25 minutes, or until the cakes are springy to the touch and a skewer inserted into the middle comes out clean.

Remove the cakes from the oven and leave to cool in the tins for 10 minutes, then turn out onto wire racks, peel off the lining paper and leave to cool completely.

You can store the cakes wrapped in plastic wrap for 3 days or in the freezer for up to a month. Defrost overnight.

Blueberry Cake

MAKES: 18 CM (7 IN) ROUND CAKE   SERVES: 8–10
PREPARATION TIME: 20 MINUTES   COOKING TIME: 45 MINUTES
COOLING TIME: 30 MINUTES

185 g (6½ oz/1¼ cups) plain (all-purpose) flour,
plus extra for coating
1 teaspoon baking powder
170 g (6 oz) fresh blueberries
185 g (6½ oz) unsalted butter, softened
185 g caster (superfine) sugar

¼ teaspoon salt
1 teaspoon natural vanilla extract
3 large eggs, separated
135 ml (4½ fl oz) full-cream (whole) milk

Preheat the oven to 180°C (350°F) and line one 18 cm (7 in) round springform cake tin with non-stick baking paper.

Sift the flour and baking powder into a bowl and set aside. Coat the blueberries with the extra flour to avoid them sinking in the cake. Set aside.

Using a standmixer, cream the butter and 150 g (5½ oz/⅔ cup) of the sugar together for 5 minutes, or until light and fluffy. Add the salt, vanilla and egg yolks and beat until creamy. Alternating, add some of the flour mixture and then some of the milk to the egg yolk mixture, until all added. Gently stir in the blueberries.

Using a standmixer, beat the egg whites to soft peaks, then slowly add the remaining sugar

until it reaches stiff peaks. Then, gently fold the egg whites into the cake mixture with a spatula, trying not to lose any air from the egg whites.

Pour the cake batter into the prepared cake tin and create a well in the centre to prevent a large hump from rising. Bake for about 45 minutes (check it after 30 minutes), or until the cake is springy to the touch and a skewer inserted into the middle comes out clean.

Remove the cake from the oven and leave to cool in the tin for 10 minutes, then turn it out onto a wire rack, peel off the lining paper and leave to cool completely.

You can store the cake wrapped in plastic wrap for 3 days or in the freezer for up to a month. Defrost overnight.

Vanilla Cupcakes
& variations

MAKES: 12 CUPCAKES
PREPARATION TIME: 30 MINUTES   COOKING TIME: 18–20 MINUTES
COOLING TIME: 10 MINUTES

225 g (8 oz/1½ cups) self-raising flour
125 g (4½ oz) unsalted butter, softened
165 g (5¾ oz/¾ cup) caster (superfine) sugar
1 teaspoon natural vanilla extract
2 large eggs, lightly beaten
125 ml (4 fl oz/½ cup) full-cream (whole) milk

Preheat the oven to 180°C (350°F) and line one 12-hole muffin tin with paper cupcake cases. Sift the flour into a bowl and set aside.

Using a standmixer, cream the butter, sugar and vanilla together for 5 minutes, or until light and fluffy. Add the beaten eggs, a little at a time, still beating with the mixer to prevent the mixture curdling. If it does separate, just add a teaspoonful of flour and continue beating, occasionally scraping down the side of the bowl with a spatula. Once the eggs and the butter are well combined, mix in the flour and milk alternately in two batches each.

Scoop the mixture into the cupcake cases, filling to two-thirds full and bake for about 18–20 minutes until the sponge is lightly golden and springs back to the touch.

Remove the tin from the oven and leave to cool for 5 minutes. Then, lift out the cupcakes and leave to cool fully on a wire rack.

You can store the cupcakes wrapped in plastic wrap for 3 days or in the freezer for up to a month. Defrost overnight.

Variations

Lemon cupcakes
Replace the natural vanilla extract with the finely grated zest of 1 lemon.

Orange cupcakes
Replace the natural vanilla extract with the finely grated zest of 1 orange.

Chocolate cupcakes
Substitute 30 g (1 oz/about ¼ cup) of flour with the same quantity of sifted cocoa powder.

Marbled vanilla & chocolate cupcakes
Make half a batch of vanilla mixture and half a batch of chocolate mixture, then fill the cupcake cases with alternating dollops of each mixture.

Vanilla Cookies
& variations

MAKES: ABOUT 30 COOKIES
CHILLING TIME: 1½ HOURS   COOKING TIME: 14–18 MINUTES
COOLING TIME: 5–10 MINUTES

400 g (14 oz/2⅔ cups) plain (all-purpose) flour,
plus extra for dusting
200 g (7 oz) unsalted butter, softened
200 g (7 oz) caster (superfine) sugar

pinch of salt
1 teaspoon natural vanilla extract
1 large egg, lightly beaten

Preheat the oven to 170°C (325°F) and line two baking trays with non-stick baking paper. Sift the flour into a bowl and set aside.

Using a standmixer, cream the butter, sugar, salt and vanilla together for 1 minute, or until smooth. Still mixing, slowly add the beaten egg until it is well incorporated into the mixture. Add the flour and mix briefly until a dough just comes together.

Shape the dough into a flat disc, wrap in plastic wrap and chill in the refrigerator for an hour, or until the dough feels firm and cool.

Remove the dough from the refrigerator, knead briefly, then place between two sheets of baking paper. Roll out to a thickness of 5 mm (¼ in). Using a selection of cookie cutters, cut out the cookies and place them on the prepared baking trays (remember always bake the same size together on a tray). Chill for 30 minutes.

Bake the cookies for 14–18 minutes, or until they are golden brown around the edges (the chocolate variation will begin to darken slightly). Cool on a wire rack.

Variations

Orange cookies
Replace the natural vanilla extract with the finely grated zest of 2 oranges.

Lemon cookies
Replace the natural vanilla extract with the finely grated zest of 3 lemons.

Chocolate cookies
Replace 30 g (1 oz/about ¼ cup) of the flour with the same quantity of sifted cocoa powder.

chapter
2

FILLINGS &
FROSTINGS

Buttercream

MAKES: ABOUT 350 G (12 OZ) TO COVER 12–16 CUPCAKES
OR FILL AND COVER ONE 18 CM (7 IN) ROUND CAKE
PREPARATION TIME: 15 MINUTES

125 g (4½ oz) unsalted butter, softened
250 g (9 oz/2 cups) icing (confectioners') sugar, sifted
2 tablespoons full-cream (whole) milk

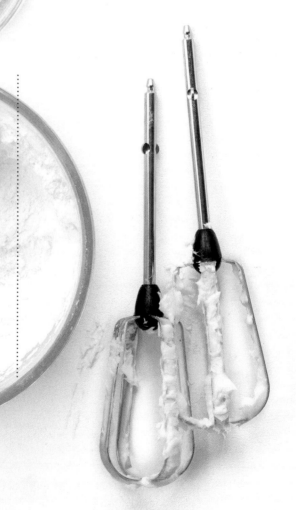

Using a standmixer, beat the butter for
5 minutes, until it is as light and creamy as
possible. Gradually add the sifted icing sugar
and the milk and beat slowly at first until
blended, then on full speed until light and fluffy.

To colour buttercream, add food colour with
a cocktail stick or toothpick and beat with a
spatula, or use a standmixer, and combine until
thoroughly blended.

Variation
Cream cheese frosting
For a cream cheese frosting add 85 g (3 oz/⅓ cup)
mascarpone cheese to the above recipe.

Buttercream will keep for up to 2 weeks,
stored in the refrigerator in an airtight
container. Bring it to room temperature first,
then beat until fluffy before using.

Royal Icing

MAKES: ABOUT 300 G (10½ OZ) TO COVER 12–16 CUPCAKES
OR COVER ONE 18 CM (7 IN) ROUND CAKE
PREPARATION TIME: 15 MINUTES

1 large egg white, at room temperature
250 g (9 oz/2 cups) icing (confectioners') sugar, sifted
½ lemon, cut into wedges

Put the egg white in a very clean mixing bowl and beat using a standmixer until it reaches soft peaks, which will take about 2–3 minutes. Add two-thirds of the sifted icing sugar and beat it in slowly at first, then on full speed for 2 minutes. Add the remaining icing sugar and whisk until stiff peaks form, which will take about 1 minute. Squeeze the lemon wedges through a tea strainer into the icing and whisk for a further minute.

To colour royal icing add food colour with a cocktail stick, toothpick or palette knife and stir the mixture thoroughly until combined.

Royal icing can be stored in an airtight container for up to a week if kept in a cool, dry place. Beat the icing well each time before use.

Sugarpaste (Ready-to-roll Fondant)

MAKES ABOUT 1.25 KG (2 LB 12 OZ) TO COVER 24 CUPCAKES OR A 20 CM (8 IN) ROUND CAKE
PREPARATION TIME: 20 MINUTES
COOKING TIME: 5 MINUTES

3 tablespoons cold water
20 g (¾ oz) powdered gelatine
125 ml (4 fl oz/½ cup) glucose syrup

3 teaspoons glycerine
1 kg (2 lb 4 oz/8 cups) icing (confectioners') sugar,
plus extra for dusting

Pour the cold water into a small heatproof bowl, sprinkle over the gelatine and soak for 2–3 minutes until spongy. Stand the bowl over a saucepan of hot but not boiling water and stir for 1 minute, or until the gelatine has dissolved. Add the glucose syrup and glycerine, stirring until well blended and runny.

Sift the icing sugar into a large bowl. Make a well in the centre and slowly pour in the liquid ingredients, stirring constantly until well mixed. Turn out onto a work surface dusted with icing sugar and knead until smooth, sprinkling with extra icing sugar if the paste becomes too sticky.

The paste can be used immediately or stored for up to 2 months if wrapped tightly in an airtight container.

TO COLOUR
SUGARPASTE
......
Dip a cocktail stick or toothpick
into your chosen colour, then
draw it across the sugarpaste
(fondant) and knead it in
thoroughly until there are
no streaks of colour left.
(See also pp 90–1.)

Dark Chocolate Ganache

and variations (on pp 48–9)

MAKES ABOUT 550 G (1 LB 4 OZ)
TO FILL AND COVER ONE 18 CM (7 IN) ROUND CAKE
WITH ENOUGH LEFT OVER FOR PIPING
PREPARATION TIME: 15 MINUTES   COOKING TIME: 2–3 MINUTES

250 g (9 oz) dark chocolate
(at least 70% cocoa), broken into pieces

250 ml (9 fl oz/1 cup) thick (double) cream
50 g (1¾ oz) unsalted butter, diced

Put the chocolate pieces into a heatproof bowl. Bring the cream just to the boil in a small saucepan over a medium heat, stirring to prevent it scorching. Pour the warm cream over the chocolate and stir until well combined. When cooled to 40°C (104°F) (test with a sugar thermometer), incorporate the butter and combine again until the ganache is rich and smooth.

Use this ganache for pouring or allow to thicken for piping.

Ganache can be stored in an airtight container in the refrigerator for up to 2 weeks or in the freezer for up to 3 months. Bring to room temperature, or warm gently in a bowl over hot water, before using.

Ganache Variations

Strawberry ganache

MAKES: ABOUT 700 G (1 LB 9 OZ) TO FILL AND COVER
  ONE 18 CM (7 IN) ROUND CAKE
PREPARATION TIME: 20 MINUTES
COOKING TIME: 5–10 MINUTES
COOLING TIME: 5 MINUTES
CHILLING TIME: AT LEAST 1 HOUR

200 g (7 oz/1⅓ cups) strawberries, hulled
  and roughly chopped
300 g (10½ oz) white chocolate, broken into pieces
150 ml (5 fl oz) thick (double) cream
30 g (1 oz) unsalted butter, diced

Cook the strawberries with 2 tablespoons water in a saucepan for 5–8 minutes over medium heat. Remove from the heat and leave to cool. Once cool, purée them using a blender until smooth.

Put the chocolate in a heatproof bowl. Bring the cream just to boiling point in a saucepan, stirring to prevent it scorching. Pour the warm cream over the chocolate and stir until well combined. When cooled to 40°C (104°F) (test with a sugar thermometer), incorporate the butter and then the strawberry coulis. Combine until the ganache is rich and smooth. Cover with plastic wrap and chill immediately in the refrigerator for at least 1 hour before using.

Pistachio ganache

MAKES: ABOUT 650 G (1 LB 7 OZ) TO FILL AND COVER
  ONE 18 CM (7 IN) ROUND CAKE
PREPARATION TIME: 15 MINUTES
COOKING TIME: 5 MINUTES
CHILLING TIME: AT LEAST 1 HOUR

300 g (10½ oz) white chocolate, broken into pieces
60 g (2¼ oz) unsalted pistachios, shelled
1–2 drops almond extract
300 ml (10½ fl oz) thick (double) cream

Put the chocolate in a heatproof bowl set over, but not touching, a saucepan of gently simmering water, and stir occasionally, until melted, about 5 minutes. Meanwhile, grind the pistachios and almond extract together very finely using a food processor until a thick paste forms. Put the paste in a saucepan, add the cream and bring just to the boil. Remove the bowl of melted chocolate from the heat, pour the warm cream over it and stir until well combined. Cover with plastic wrap and chill immediately in the refrigerator for at least 1 hour before using.

Lemon ganache

MAKES: ABOUT 650 G (1 LB 7 OZ) TO FILL AND COVER
  ONE 18 CM (7 IN) ROUND CAKE
PREPARATION TIME: 15 MINUTES
COOKING TIME: 5 MINUTES
CHILLING TIME: AT LEAST 1 HOUR

225 g (8 oz) white chocolate, broken into pieces
100 ml (3½ fl oz) lemon juice
finely grated zest of 1 lemon

Put the chocolate in a heatproof bowl set over, but not touching, a saucepan of gently simmering water, and stir occasionally, until melted, about 5 minutes. Meanwhile, pour the lemon juice into a small saucepan and bring to the boil. Remove the bowl of chocolate from the heat, pour the lemon juice over it and stir until well combined. Add the lemon zest and combine until the ganache is smooth. Cover with plastic wrap and chill immediately in the refrigerator for at least 1 hour before using.

Dark Chocolate Modelling Paste (Plastique)

MAKES: ABOUT 550 G (1 LB 4 OZ) TO COVER ONE 18 CM (7 IN) ROUND CAKE
PREPARATION TIME: 15 MINUTES   COOKING TIME: 5 MINUTES
SETTING TIME: OVERNIGHT

300 g (10½ oz) chocolate buttons
(at least 55% cocoa)
250 ml (9 fl oz/1 cup) glucose syrup

Put the chocolate in a heatproof bowl set over, but not touching, a saucepan of gently simmering water, and stir occasionally, until melted, about 2–3 minutes, and it has reached 40°C (104°F) (test with a sugar thermometer). Clean the thermometer. In another saucepan, heat the glucose syrup until it reaches 40°C (104°F) on the sugar thermometer, about 2–3 minutes. Add the chocolate to the syrup and stir it to a thick paste. Wrap in plastic wrap and leave overnight at room temperature to set.

Knead the modelling paste on a work surface lightly dusted with icing (confectioners') sugar until smooth and pliable. It is now ready to use.

Chocolate modelling paste can be wrapped in plastic wrap and stored at room temperature for up to 3 months.

Italian Meringue

MAKES: ABOUT 400 G (14 OZ) TO COVER ONE 20 CM (8 IN) ROUND CAKE
PREPARATION TIME: 15 MINUTES
COOKING TIME: 5 MINUTES

235 g (8½ oz) caster (superfine) sugar
4 egg whites (about 120 g/4¼ oz)

Put the sugar and 100 ml (3½ fl oz) water into a small saucepan, along with a sugar thermometer. Bring to the boil over medium heat and boil until it reaches 118–120°C (244–248°F), known as soft-ball stage.

Using a standmixer, whisk the egg whites on low speed until they become foamy, then gradually add the sugar syrup in a steady stream, whisking constantly until the meringue is very firm and glossy.

The meringue must be used immediately.

Coffee Cream

MAKES: ABOUT 450 G (1 LB) TO FILL AND COVER
ONE 18 CM (7 IN) ROUND CAKE
PREPARATION TIME: 15 MINUTES

115 g (4 oz) unsalted butter, softened
340 g (12 oz/2¾ cups) icing (confectioners') sugar
50 ml (1¾ fl oz) freshly made black coffee

Beat the butter in a bowl using a standmixer for 5 minutes, or until smooth and fluffy. Gradually add the icing sugar and coffee, beat slowly at first on low speed until blended, then on full speed until light and fluffy.

Use immediately or store in an airtight container in the refrigerator.

chapter
3

LAYERING,
COVERING
& STACKING

Layer, Fill & Cover with Buttercream

In order to layer a multi-tiered cake you will first need to 'tort' it,
which refers to the technique used to cut a cake into various layers.
(Step 2 of this method teaches you how to do this.)

1/// Using a serrated knife and holding it flat, trim the top off the cake. Put the cake upside down and score a V-shape all the way down one edge so you can line it back up again when you put the pieces together.

2/// Tort the cake by first tracing two lines around the sides and then slicing right across starting with the top line.

3/// Secure the bottom layer of the cake to a cake board with a dollop of filling smeared directly onto the board and brush the cake with syrup using a pastry brush.

4/// Place a dollop of buttercream in the centre of the cake and spread evenly to the edge with a palette knife and repeat the whole process for the other layer.

5/// To avoid crumbs on the final frosting, apply a thin layer of buttercream to the top and side of the cake to create a crumb coat. Leave it to set for 15 minutes in the refrigerator before applying the next layer.

6/// Put a large dollop of buttercream on top of the cake and spread evenly. Do the same for the side and then, using a long spatula, remove the excess buttercream to leave a smooth surface.

Cover with Sugarpaste (Fondant)

Once layered and secured to a cake board, your cake is ready to
be covered. A single tier can simply be covered with sugarpaste,
while a multi-tiered cake should have marzipan applied first.

1/// Lightly dust the work surface with icing
(confectioners') sugar, knead the sugarpaste
(ready-to-roll fondant) until smooth and pliable,
then roll it to a thickness of approximately
5 mm (¼ in).

2/// Brush the cake all over with cooled boiled
water. Carefully lift the sugarpaste with both
hands directly underneath so it rests over your
hands, wrists and lower arms, then place it over
the cake. When the centre is directly over the
middle of the cake, carefully lay it over the top.

3/// Using your hands, work quickly to shape
the sugarpaste on the top, working from the
centre outwards, and then the side of the cake.

4/// Run over the top and side of the cake with
a straight-edged smoother until the surface of
the sugarpaste is completely smooth.

5/// Trim the excess of sugarpaste with a pizza
cutter around the edge of the base.

6/// Smooth over the top, side and edge of the
cake until you are happy with the finish. The
cake is now ready to be decorated.

FOR A SQUARE CAKE

*For a square cake, after you have
placed the sugarpaste over the cake,
pull the corner flaps gently out and
away from the cake. Smooth the
corners with your hands to eliminate
any creases, then trim the edges
and smooth the top and sides with
a straight-edged smoother.*

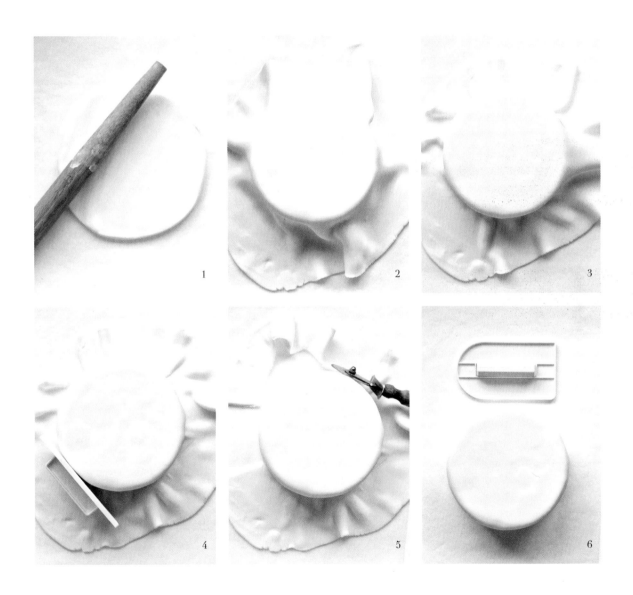

Cover with Chocolate Ganache

Slightly warmed chocolate ganache makes a delightful finish.
It can be poured over a cake that has already been layered
and secured to a cake board.

1/// Cover the top and side of the cake with a thin layer of a slightly set chocolate ganache to create a crumb coat. Set aside for 15 minutes.

2/// Place the cake on a wire rack over a sheet of non-stick baking paper. Warm the remaining ganache over a bain-marie, stirring, until it is glossy and smooth, then pour it over the cake.

3/// Once the ganache has been poured over the top and side of the cake, smooth the surface using a palette knife.

4/// Carefully lift the wire rack and tap it gently against the work surface to even out the ganache and ensure that the cake is covered.

Ganache
Tip

★

Ganache can also be used to make decorations if it is left to thicken.

1

2

3

4

Decorating Cupcakes with Buttercream

WIDE STAR NOZZLE

To use the wide star nozzle to create a swirl, pipe buttercream from the outside to the centre ending with a point.

CLOSED STAR NOZZLE

Use the closed star nozzle to pipe buttercream in circles from the inside to the outside to form a rose.

Using buttercream to decorate cupcakes is a quick and easy way to give them a professional-looking finish. Various piping nozzles and techniques can be used to achieve different results.

WIDE ROUND NOZZLE

Using a wide round nozzle, pipe buttercream into the centre of the cupcake to form a large blob.

PALETTE KNIFE

Squeeze out a small amount of buttercream and use a palette knife to spread it sideways around the top of the cupcake.

Filling Cupcakes

You can really have fun with flavour when you add a tasty filling to your baked cupcakes. Here are two ways to do this.

USING A BISMARCK NOZZLE

Prepare a piping (icing) bag with a Bismarck nozzle (or a piping tube nozzle) and your desired filling. Insert the pointed tip into an un-iced cupcake and gently squeeze out a small amount of your chosen filling to fill the cupcake. Ice as desired.

USING AN APPLE CORER

Remove the centre of an un-iced cupcake with an apple corer and cut the top off the removed centre. Squeeze out a small amount of your chosen filling into the cupcake and cover with the top of the centre piece. Ice as desired.

Hidden Treasure

For a delightful surprise hidden inside your cupcakes, follow this
simple method to create coloured centres.

Colour a small batch of the cake mixture in your chosen colour, then spread it out on a baking tray and cook in an oven preheated to 180°C (350°F) for around 15 minutes.

Using a small cookie cutter, cut out some shapes from the cooked mixture. Line a muffin tin with paper cupcake cases and place the cooked shapes in the centre of the cases. Carefully spoon in the remaining uncooked cake mixture to enclose the cooked shapes.

Bake for about 18–20 minutes, cool and then decorate to your liking.

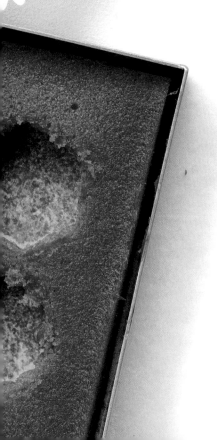

Covering Cupcakes with Poured Royal Icing

Cupcakes can be given a fun finish simply by pouring coloured royal icing over the top. For a vibrant plate of cupcakes, use a variety of colours.

Make sure the cupcakes rise to just under the top of the paper cupcake cases to leave space for the icing. Make a batch of royal icing (to add colour, see page 42), then slowly pour it onto the cupcakes until it almost reaches the top of the paper cases.

Tap the cupcakes on the work surface to remove any air bubbles and then quickly add any decorations such as flowers, if using. Otherwise, let the icing dry before piping a decoration.

Stacking a Cake with Dowels

When creating a multi-tiered cake it is important to ensure that the bottom layer is supported well with dowels, otherwise the weight of the other layers can cause it to collapse.

1/// Place the base cake on a work surface and then position a cake board that is the same size as the next cake tier in the middle of the base cake. Press down to make a slight impression in the icing before removing the cake board.

2/// Insert 4–6 dowels (depending on the cake size) into the base cake, pushing down until they reach the work surface. Mark the dowels with a pencil in line with the iced surface.

3/// Remove the dowels, then cut around the marks using a sharp knife. Place the dowels back into position in the base cake, and smooth a little royal icing over the tops of them using a palette knife.

4/// Lift up the top cake tier with a palette knife and carefully position it onto the cake below.

chapter
4

PIPING
TECHNIQUES

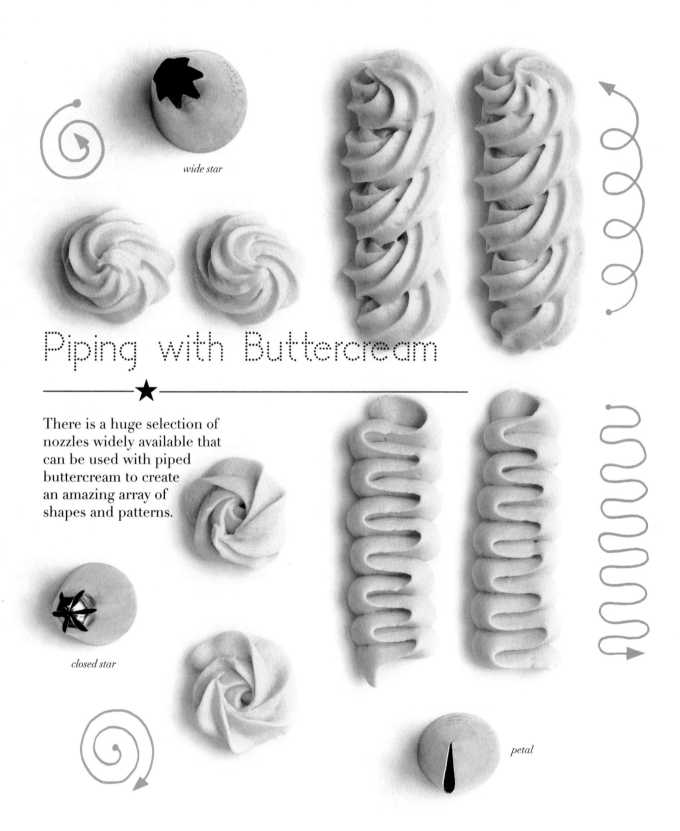

wide star

Piping with Buttercream

★

There is a huge selection of nozzles widely available that can be used with piped buttercream to create an amazing array of shapes and patterns.

closed star

petal

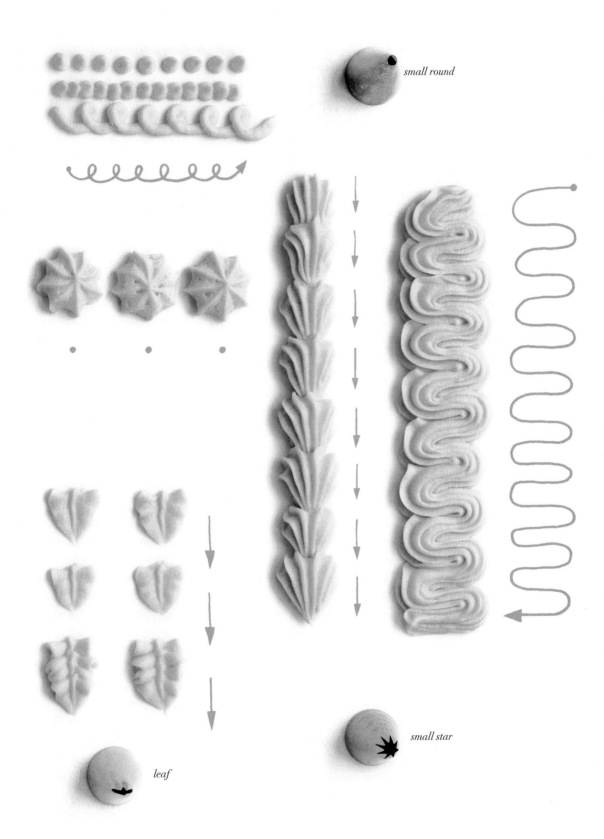

small round

leaf

small star

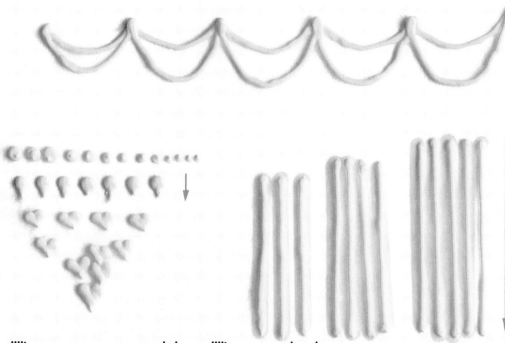

Piping with Royal Icing

★

Royal icing is used to
create delicate decorations
such as small hearts,
flowers and leaves, and
intricate techniques like
brush embroidery
and cornelli lace.

*small round
(number 1)*

brush embroidery

cornelli lace

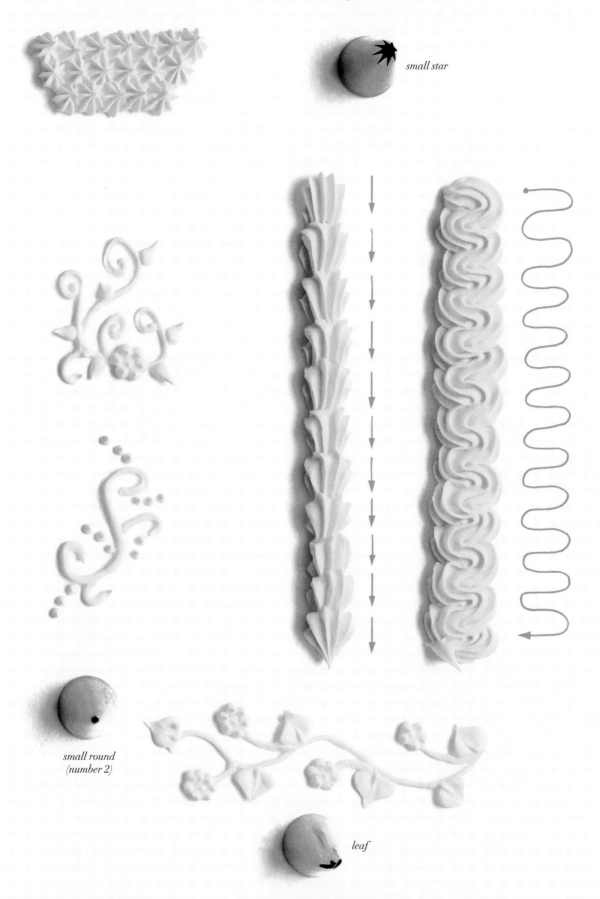

small star

small round
(number 2)

leaf

Flowers

★

Making drop flowers out of buttercream is really simple and quick. You can pipe drop flowers directly onto your cake and cupcakes, or you can pipe them in advance and place the flowers later.

Prepare a piping (icing) bag with a 2D (Wilton) nozzle or a closed star nozzle and another bag with a number 3 round nozzle and fill them with coloured buttercream of your choice.

DROP STAR FLOWER

Hold the piping bag straight up with the nozzle lightly touching the surface, squeeze and let the buttercream build up to make the flower, then stop and lift away. For the flower centre, hold the other piping bag straight up and squeeze out the buttercream to build the dot.

squeeze and lift

DROP SWIRL FLOWER

Touch the surface lightly with the nozzle, and, as you squeeze out the buttercream, slowly turn your hand, then stop and lift the piping bag away. For the flower centre, hold the other piping bag straight up and squeeze out the buttercream to build the dot.

squeeze, turn and lift

Aa Bb Cc

Gg Hh Ii

Mm Nn Oo

Ss Tt Uu

Yy Zz

Gâteau Bolo

Tourta

Tàrta

You can have great fun creating personalised cakes by writing on them.
But a beautifully decorated cake can be ruined by uneven or messy writing.
Ensure you add a few drops of piping gel or water to thin the icing –
and practise a lot beforehand on a different surface!

heart

lips

smiley face

Christmas tree

balloon

butterfly

star

ghost

musical notes

apple

mushroom

iceblock
(popsicle/ice lolly)

Royal Icing Decorations

★

Royal icing decorations are perfect for adding embellishments to cakes and cupcakes. They can be made months in advance – but at least one day before you are planning to use them. Piped directly onto non-stick baking paper, the decorations are made up of layers of royal icing, the consistency of which should be soft peak in order to hold the shapes when piped.

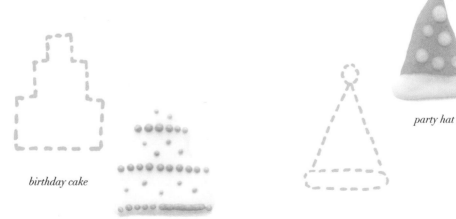

birthday cake

party hat

Piping Borders

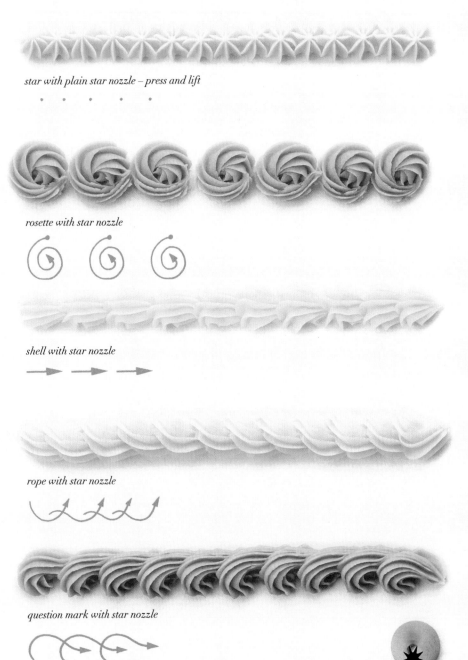

star with plain star nozzle – press and lift

rosette with star nozzle

shell with star nozzle

rope with star nozzle

question mark with star nozzle

By piping borders you can turn a simple cake into a very beautiful and elegant one. There are various simple borders that are easy to master and the size and shape of each one will vary depending on the nozzle. All you need is practice to become familiar with the amount of pressure required as you pipe.

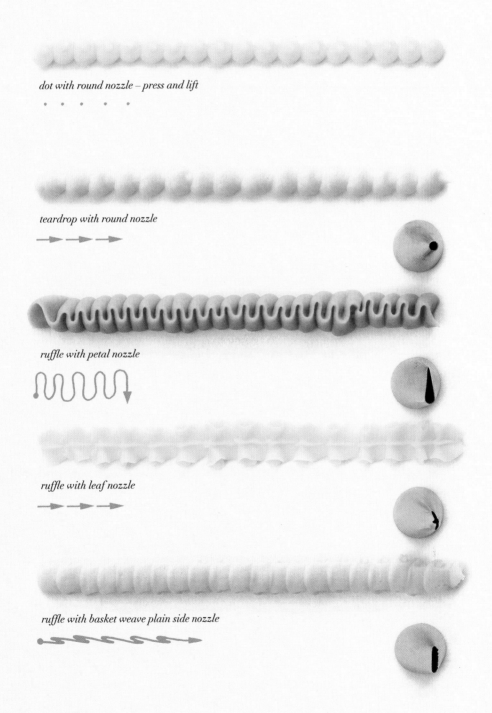

dot with round nozzle – press and lift

teardrop with round nozzle

ruffle with petal nozzle

ruffle with leaf nozzle

ruffle with basket weave plain side nozzle

chapter
5

DECORATING
WITH
SUGARPASTE

Mixing Colours

red + blue = purple

blue + yellow = green

yellow + red = orange

red + green = brown

yellow + green = light green

It is easy to mix different sugarpaste (fondant) colours together to achieve any shade or depth of colour. Here's a quick guide to mixing colours.

blue + green = turquoise or blue-green

red + white = pink

blue + pink = mauve

white + black = grey

blue + white = sky blue

Plunger Cutters

1/// Lightly dust a work surface with icing (confectioners') sugar, knead and soften the sugarpaste (fondant) and then roll it out to a thickness of 3 mm (⅛ in).

2/// Hold the plunger by the base and cut the shape. Place the cutter (and attached shape) onto the work surface and press the plunger to indent the details.

3/// Lift the plunger cutter and press to release the shape. Let it dry before using it to decorate the cake, cupcake or cookie.

Cut-out Cutters

1/// Lightly dust a work surface with icing (confectioners') sugar, knead and soften the sugarpaste (fondant) and then roll it out to a thickness of 3 mm (⅛ in).

2/// With your chosen cutter push down firmly onto the sugarpaste and gently move the cutter back and forth to ensure it cuts all the way through the sugarpaste.

3/// Peel away the extra sugarpaste and leave the shapes to firm up before removing them with a palette knife and using to decorate the cake, cupcakes or cookies.

Cutters

Using cutters to create shapes is an easy and quick way
to add decoration to cakes, cupcakes and cookies.

Layering Shapes

1/// Lightly dust a work surface with icing (confectioners') sugar, knead and soften the different coloured sugarpaste (fondant), then roll them out to a thickness of 3 mm (⅛ in).

2/// Cut out the sugarpaste in different sizes and shapes following the instructions given on pages 92–3.

3/// Once the shapes are slightly dry, arrange them one layer at a time on top of each other, securing them with edible glue.

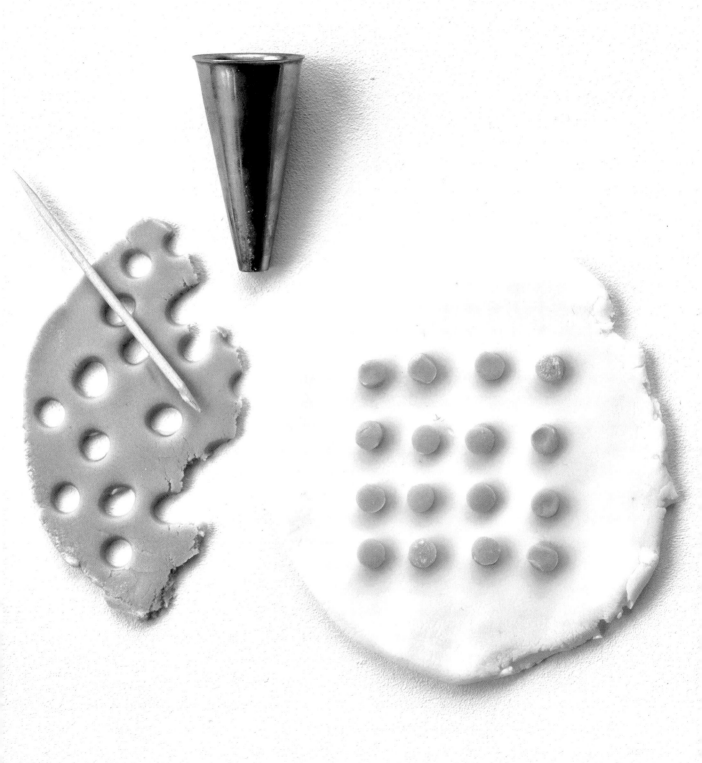

Repeat Patterns

Colour a small batch of the sugarpaste (fondant) green and roll it out to a thickness of 3 mm (⅛ in) on a work surface lightly dusted with icing (confectioners') sugar.

Roll out the background sugarpaste so that it is slightly thicker than the contrasting coloured paste.

Cut out shapes from the coloured sugarpaste with a cutter and place them over the background paste.

Roll over in all directions to get back to the original thickness.

Silicone 3D Mould: 1 Colour

1/// Lightly dust a decorative silicone mould with icing (confectioners') sugar. Knead small amounts of coloured sugarpaste (fondant), roll each into a ball and place into the mould cavities.

2/// Push the sugarpaste down to ensure the deeper sections of the mould are filled and scrape off the excess with a palette knife.

3/// Hold the mould with both hands and press the centre of each shape with your thumb to release the sugarpaste.

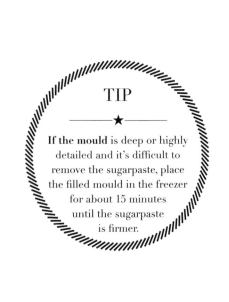

TIP

★

If the mould is deep or highly detailed and it's difficult to remove the sugarpaste, place the filled mould in the freezer for about 15 minutes until the sugarpaste is firmer.

Silicone 3D Mould: 2 Colours

1/// Lightly dust a decorative silicone mould with icing (confectioners') sugar. Knead a small amount of coloured sugarpaste (fondant), roll into a ball smaller than the space you want to fill and place it into the cavity.

Ensure that the sugarpaste just lines this section so that it won't spread when the next colour is added.

2/// Knead a small amount of sugarpaste of another colour, press into the mould and scrape off the excess with a palette knife.

3/// Hold the mould with both hands and press the centre of each shape with your thumb to release the sugarpaste.

TIP

★

If the coloured centre has spread to the surrounding area, you need to put less sugarpaste in the centre next time.

Simple Flowers

CALLA LILY

1/// Colour the sugarpaste (fondant) appropriately and roll to a thickness of 2 mm (1⁄16 in). Cut out a white heart and a green circle, place on a foam pad and use a ball tool to thin the edges.

2/// Place the heart around a nozzle and fold the two arches over each other. Brush with edible glue to secure them.

3/// Cut the green circle in half and wrap one piece around the base of the lily, using edible glue to secure it. Using your fingertips, gently curl the edge of the petal. Let it dry.

4/// Roll a small amount of yellow sugarpaste into a thin log, brush the inside of the lily with edible glue and insert the yellow log into the centre, gently pressing to secure.

CUPPED FLOWER

1/// Lightly dust the work surface with some icing (confectioners') sugar, knead and soften the coloured sugarpaste (fondant) and roll it out to a thickness of 2 mm (1⁄16 in). To make the petals, cut out six round shapes.

2/// Place the round shapes on a foam pad and use a ball tool to stroke around the edges in order to soften and frill them.

3/// Make a mould by pushing a piece of non-stick baking paper into a round cookie cutter. Place the petals in so that they overlap, use edible glue to secure them and let them dry.

4/// To make the flower centre, add small white sugarpaste balls and secure them with edible glue.

RUFFLE FLOWER

1/// Knead and soften the sugarpaste (fondant), then roll it out to a thickness of 2 mm (1/16 in). Cut out five circles with a diameter of 5 cm (2 in).

2/// Dust the circles with icing (confectioners') sugar then fold each one in half, then in half again, pinching only in the centre so that the edges do not touch. Leave to dry.

3/// Assemble the first four folded circles together so that the pointed corners are all in the centre, touching inwards. Secure them with edible glue.

4/// To finish the flower, brush the tops of the four circles with edible glue and position the last folded circle in the middle.

ROSEBUD

1/// Lightly dust the work surface with some icing (confectioners') sugar, knead and soften the sugarpaste (fondant). Reserve a small ball off to the side. Roll the rest to a thickness of 2 mm (1/16 in). Cut out a flower with a 5-petal flower cutter.

2/// Place the flower on a foam pad and thin the edges with a ball tool. Make a cone shape from the reserved sugarpaste ball and place in the centre with some edible glue.

3/// Brush some edible glue onto the first petal and pull it up to cover the cone, wrapping it around. Do the same with a petal on the opposite side to make the central bud.

4/// Continue to wrap the remaining three petals over the central bud, using edible glue to secure the rosebud shape and then leave it to dry.

Hand-moulded Daffodils

1/// Colour the majority of the sugarpaste (fondant) yellow, but colour some of it orange for the trumpets.

Lightly dust the work surface with some icing (confectioners') sugar. Roll out the yellow sugarpaste to a thickness of 2 mm (1⁄16 in). Cut out two star shapes with a calyx cutter.

2/// Make some indentions on the petals with a blade tool. Brush the centre of one shape with edible glue, then place the other on top diagonally across it and push down.

3/// To create the trumpet, make a cone with the orange sugarpaste and form the centre with a cone tool. Fix it into the centre of the flower with some edible glue and then curl the petals slightly around it.

Leave to dry before using.

Hand-moulded Poppies

1/// Colour the majority of the sugarpaste (fondant) red, but colour some of it black for the poppy centres.

Lightly dust a work surface with some icing (confectioners') sugar. Roll out the red sugarpaste to a thickness of 2 mm (1/16 in). Cut out two shapes with a 5-petal flower cutter per flower.

2/// Place the shapes on a foam pad and use a ball tool to gently thin the edges in order to shape and form all the petals of each flower.

3/// Set one flower in a small bowl to curve it, place the second flower diagonally across so that the petals of the second flower are in between the petals of the first flower and attach with edible glue. Curl up the edges of the petals.

Roll a small ball out of the black sugarpaste, flatten slightly and secure it in the centre of the flower with edible glue. Use a cocktail stick or toothpick to indent over the surface of the black centre. Leave the poppy to dry before using.

Hand-moulded Roses

1/// Colour the sugarpaste (fondant). Roll it into a sausage shape (1 cm/½ in diameter for small roses) on a work surface lightly dusted with icing sugar. Trim an end and cut off six discs that are 3–4 mm (⅛ in) thick.

2/// When you cut the sausage shape, the bottom part, which is in contact with the work surface, will flatten slightly. Place the cut discs in a plastic document holder with the straight edge down.

3/// To shape the petals flatten the discs slightly with the palm of your hand and then use your thumb to smooth all around the curved edge. Try to work quickly to prevent them drying out.

4/// Release one of the petals from the plastic and make the centre of the rose by curling the petal horizontally and gently rolling it into a tight cone.

5/// Release the next petal off the plastic and lay the join of the first petal with the middle of the second petal with the top just slightly higher. Gently pinch the bottom of the second petal in.

6/// Repeat the same process with the third petal, laying the join of the second petal in the centre of the third petal and pinch around the base.

7/// Position the other three petals in exactly the same way but creating one row by overlapping each of them around the outside of the rose.

8/// To finish the rose, use a sharp knife to slice off the chunky base of sugarpaste and set aside to dry before using.

Hand-moulded Peonies

1/// Colour the sugarpaste (fondant). Roll it out to a thickness of 2 mm (1/16 in) on a work surface lightly dusted with some icing (confectioners') sugar. Cut out two shapes with a large 5-petal flower cutter (for each flower).

2/// Place the flowers on a foam pad, cut a V-shape on both sides of each petal and smooth the edges with a ball tool.

3/// Make some slight indentions with a blade tool to give a double petal effect (like you did with the daffodils, see page 106).

4/// Set one flower in a small bowl to curve it, place the second flower diagonally across so that the petals of the second flower are in between the petals of the first flower and attach with edible glue.

5/// To create the inside petals, cut out three small round shapes with a frill cutter.

6/// With the end of a paintbrush, roll over the edges of the round shapes with a backwards and forwards motion to create a ruffle.

7/// Pinch the base of each to create the finished inside petals.

8/// Place the inside petals in the centre of the outer petals brushing with edible glue. Adjust the position of the petals to give a natural look.

Making Simple Animals

STARFISH

1/// Colour the sugarpaste (fondant). Knead and soften the sugarpaste, then roll out each colour to a thickness of 5 mm (¼ in) and cut out a star shape.

2/// Using your fingertips, smooth the points and the sharp edges, and gently shape the arms.

3/// With a leaf shaper tool, make an indention in each place that the arms join together.

4/// To add texture to each starfish, use the same tool to prick tiny dots down the centre of each arm.

DRAGONFLY

1/// Colour the sugarpaste (fondant). Roll out the blue to a thickness of 2 mm (1/16 in). Cut out two flowers, one slightly bigger, with a 5-petal flower cutter. Roll a medium ball of the green and two little balls with the white and leftover blue.

2/// For the wings, cut off two petals from each flower, place them on a foam pad and use a ball tool to work around the edges to make them thinner.

3/// Make a long green log, ensuring one end is thinner than the other. Mark some indentions using a blade tool. Divide the white and blue balls in two, flatten slightly and with the ball tool position them on the front of the head (the wide end of the green log).

4/// Place the two big wings at the front and the two small wings at the back. Brush them with edible glue and position the body on top. Use a scallop tool to indent a smile on the face.

BUTTERFLY

1/// Colour the sugarpaste (fondant). Knead and soften the sugarpaste, reserve a medium ball and roll the rest to a thickness of 5 mm (¼ in). Cut out the butterflies with a butterfly cutter.

2/// Using the sugarpaste ball you set aside, roll four long sausage shapes and make a cut at one end of each with a blade tool. With a small round nozzle, add some decoration to the butterfly wings.

3/// Place the butterfly shapes on a flower former to shape and dry them.

4/// Use edible glue to attach the body to each butterfly. Let the glue dry before using the butterflies.

SWAN

1/// Colour the sugarpaste (fondant). Roll a big and a medium white ball. Shape the big ball so it is slightly pointed (for the body) and the medium into a question mark (for the neck). Shape a cone from a small yellow ball and flatten a tiny black ball. Roll out some more white sugarpaste to a thickness of 2 mm (¹⁄₁₆ in) and cut out two wing shapes.

2/// To make the head, use edible glue to attach the flattened black ball to the top of the neck and then position the yellow cone so that you cover the majority of the black sugarpaste on the bottom.

3/// Emboss some feathery patterns on the wings using a shell tool, then use edible glue to attach them to the body, ensuring that the pointed ends are positioned at what will be the front of the swan.

4/// Position the end of the neck under the body and secure it with edible glue. Use a cocktail stick or toothpick dipped in black food colouring to make the eyes.

Hand-moulded Bumblebee & Ladybird

FOR THE BUMBLEBEE

FOR THE LADYBIRD

1/// Colour some of the sugarpaste (fondant) yellow. Fit a piping (icing) bag with a number 2 round nozzle and fill with white royal icing and another bag with black royal icing.

Roll a small piece of yellow sugarpaste into a small sausage. Roll out the white sugarpaste to a thickness of 5 mm (¼ in) on a work surface lightly dusted with icing (confectioners') sugar. Cut out a shape with a 5-petal flower cutter and use two of the petals for wings.

2/// Paint three stripes on the body with black food colouring. Attach the wings with edible glue. Mark a smile on the front of the body with a scallop tool and pipe two dots with the white royal icing for eyes.

Let the icing dry for 10 minutes before adding a small black dot to each eye with the black royal icing. Leave to set before using.

1/// Colour the sugarpaste (fondant) red.

Fit a piping (icing) bag with a number 2 round nozzle and fill it with white royal icing.

For each ladybird, roll a piece of red sugarpaste into a small sausage and mark a line along the length.

2/// Paint six black spots on the ladybird's back with black food colouring. Paint the face on one end and pipe two small white pearls of royal icing on top for the eyes.

Leave the ladybird to dry before using.

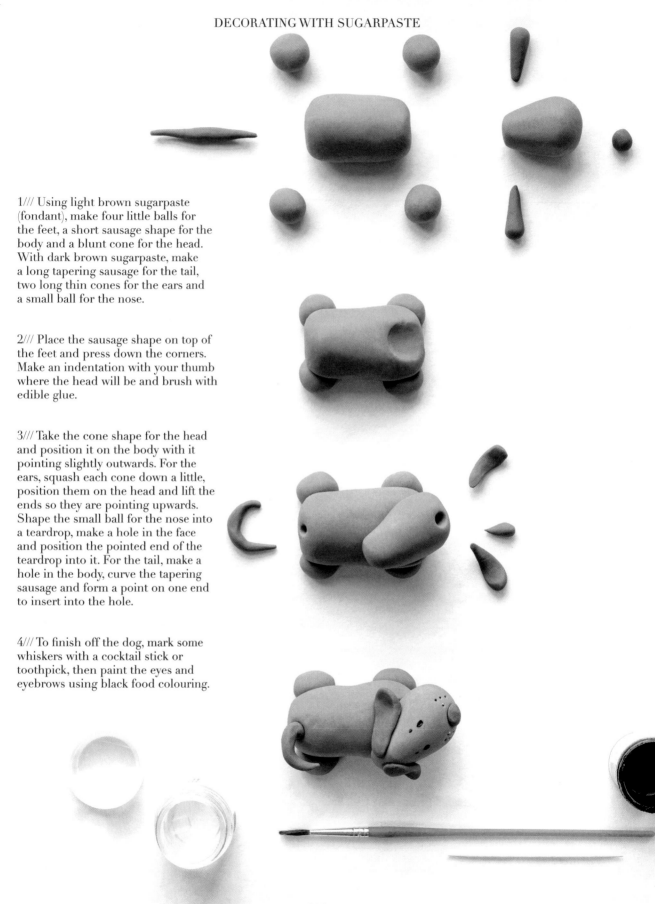

1/// Using light brown sugarpaste (fondant), make four little balls for the feet, a short sausage shape for the body and a blunt cone for the head. With dark brown sugarpaste, make a long tapering sausage for the tail, two long thin cones for the ears and a small ball for the nose.

2/// Place the sausage shape on top of the feet and press down the corners. Make an indentation with your thumb where the head will be and brush with edible glue.

3/// Take the cone shape for the head and position it on the body with it pointing slightly outwards. For the ears, squash each cone down a little, position them on the head and lift the ends so they are pointing upwards. Shape the small ball for the nose into a teardrop, make a hole in the face and position the pointed end of the teardrop into it. For the tail, make a hole in the body, curve the tapering sausage and form a point on one end to insert into the hole.

4/// To finish off the dog, mark some whiskers with a cocktail stick or toothpick, then paint the eyes and eyebrows using black food colouring.

Hand-moulded Dog

1/// Colour most of the sugarpaste (fondant) brown. Make a large blunt teardrop for the body, an oval shape for the head and four teardrops for the legs and arms, making the arms a little longer. Use a small amount of brown sugarpaste for the snout·and create two small teardrops for the ears. Using a small amount of black sugarpaste, make three little balls for the eyes and the nose.

2/// To create the teddy's legs, pinch the wide part of each teardrop to shape it into a foot. Pressing to flatten, attach the snout and then the nose and eyes onto the head using edible glue.

3/// Position the body onto the legs and attach the arms, curving them around, to either side of the body using edible glue. Now gently insert a short piece of spaghetti into the bear's body. Make two holes towards the top of the head with the end of a paintbrush and fit the ears into these, squashing them slightly once they are in place.

4/// Indent a smile on the snout with a scallop tool. Carefully lower the head onto the spaghetti and attach it to the body using edible glue. Leave the teddy to dry before placing it on your cake or cupcake.

Hand-moulded Teddy Bear

Hand-moulded Shapes

Sugarpaste (ready-to-roll fondant) is ideal to use when making hand-moulded decorations. It can be used to make elegant flowers, and sugarpaste animals can be as simple or as complicated as you want to make them, but many will have basic shapes in common.

chapter
6

CAKE
PROJECTS

Ombre Cake

PROJECT COMPLEXITY: 🧁🧁

YOU WILL NEED: *Ombre cake (see page 22);*
Buttercream (see page 40)

CAKE PREPARATION TIME: 1½ HOURS
BUTTERCREAM PREPARATION TIME: 15 MINUTES
DECORATING TIME: 50 MINUTES

Applying a crumb coat to the layered cake.

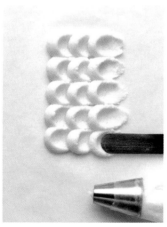

Creating a scalloped effect.

Prepare the cakes by removing the crust on the side with a serrated knife (see page 58), filling and then layering them.

Apply a crumb coat (see page 58) and leave to set for 30 minutes.

Fit a disposable piping (icing) bag with a round nozzle and fill it with vanilla buttercream (see page 15). To achieve a scalloped effect on the cake edge, pipe a line of five dots, then smear each dot to the right using the end of a palette knife. (Clean the palette knife after each dot.) Pipe a second line of dots to the right and halfway over the first line, smear them and continue to pipe to cover the whole side of the cake. Start piping the top with the same technique in a spiral formation, starting from the outside and working your way inwards.

Lemon & Poppy Seed Drizzle Cake

PROJECT COMPLEXITY:

YOU WILL NEED: *two quantities Lemon & poppy seed drizzle cake (see page 24); Italian meringue (see page 52); two quantities Sugarpaste (see page 44)*

CAKE PREPARATION TIME: 1 HOUR 40 MINUTES
ITALIAN MERINGUE PREPARATION TIME: 20 MINUTES   SUGARPASTE PREPARATION TIME: 25 MINUTES
DECORATING TIME: 30 MINUTES

Cut out small circles of assorted colours.

Using edible glue, attach the circles to the cake.

After filling the cake with the Italian meringue and covering it with sugarpaste (fondant) (see page 60), prepare the decoration by cutting out circles of rolled sugarpaste in assorted colours with a small round cutter.

Apply some edible glue to the back of each circle and then carefully place it onto the side of the cake, starting with the top cake tier. Press gently to fix it to the cake. Continue this process until the whole cake is decorated.

Chocolate Truffle Cake
with Chocolate Ganache
& Chocolate Modelling Paste

PROJECT COMPLEXITY:

YOU WILL NEED: *Chocolate truffle cake (see page 20); Chocolate ganache (see page 46); Chocolate modelling paste (see page 50); berries, for decoration*

CAKE PREPARATION TIME: 1 HOUR 45 MINUTES
CHOCOLATE GANACHE PREPARATION TIME: 18 MINUTES
CHOCOLATE MODELLING PASTE PREPARATION TIME: 20 MINUTES + OVERNIGHT
SETTING DECORATING TIME: 10 MINUTES

Creating the scalloped edge.

Position so the scalloped edge is above the cake.

Prepare the cake by first cutting out a mini cake from the big cake. Then fill this hole with chocolate ganache. On a work surface lightly dusted with icing (confectioners') sugar, roll out the chocolate modelling paste to be long enough to wrap around the cake and also be 1 cm (½ in) higher than the cake.

Cut one edge of the modelling paste straight and create a gentle scallop shape on the other using a pizza cutter.

Position the modelling paste around the cake with the straight edge flush with the base. Mould the top edge to create a sense of movement.

Decorate the top of the cake with berries and tie string around the middle if you like.

Coffee & Walnut Cake
with Coffee Cream

PROJECT COMPLEXITY: 🧁

YOU WILL NEED: *Coffee & walnut cake (see page 26); Coffee syrup (see page 26);*
Coffee cream (see page 54); walnut pieces, for decoration

CAKE PREPARATION TIME: 1 HOUR 40 MINUTES
COFFEE CREAM PREPARATION TIME: 15 MINUTES
DECORATING TIME: 10 MINUTES

Brush the cake with coffee syrup.

Brush the bottom cake with the coffee syrup.

Fit a disposable piping (icing) bag with a
star nozzle (see page 15), then fill it with
the coffee cream. Pipe this over the top
of the bottom cake.

Top with the second cake, and brush this with
coffee syrup before spreading a layer
of coffee cream on top.

Decorate the top of the cake with walnuts.

Pipe coffee cream onto the top of the bottom cake.

Orange Polenta Cake
with Pistachio Ganache

PROJECT COMPLEXITY:

YOU WILL NEED: *two quantities Orange polenta cake (see page 28);
Pistachio ganache (see page 48); three quantities Cream cheese frosting (see page 40)*

CAKE PREPARATION TIME: 1 HOUR 35 MINUTES
PISTACHIO GANACHE PREPARATION TIME: 1 HOUR 20 MINUTES
CREAM CHEESE FROSTING PREPARATION TIME: 15 MINUTES
DECORATING TIME: 50 MINUTES

Use a palette knife to apply the frosting strips.

Smooth the frosting with the palette knife.

After filling the cakes with the pistachio ganache apply a crumb coat (see page 58) and leave to set for 30 minutes.

Make three quantities of cream cheese frosting and divide it among four bowls. Colour three of the frostings with different shades of green and leave one plain.

Apply the frosting to the side of the cake in strips using a palette knife, starting with the darkest colour at the base and finishing with plain white for the last 2 cm (¾ in) and the top.

With a palette knife first smooth the cake and then with the tip make an indention all the way around starting from the top.

Decorate the top of the cake with small coloured flags if you like.

Red Velvet Cake
with Cream Cheese Frosting

PROJECT COMPLEXITY:

YOU WILL NEED: *Red velvet cake (see page 30);*
Cream cheese frosting (see page 40)

CAKE PREPARATION TIME: 1 HOUR 30 MINUTES
CREAM CHEESE FROSTING PREPARATION TIME: 15 MINUTES
DECORATING TIME: 30 MINUTES

Level the tops of the cakes with a serrated knife and keep the removed sponge, breaking it into crumbs (it will become the crumble on top).

Fit a piping (icing) bag with a wide round nozzle and spoon in some cream cheese frosting (see page 15). Pipe two layers of frosting on a cake in a spiral motion from inside to outside. Repeat for the other cake layers, placing one on top of another as you do so.

Fit the piping bag with a petal nozzle and spoon in more cream cheese frosting. Position the nozzle so the broad end touches the bottom of the cake and the narrow end faces you. Squeeze out the frosting while moving the piping bag right and left quickly as you move vertically up until you have piped a strip of ruffles. Continue to pipe until the whole cake has been covered.

Sprinkle the sponge crumble on top.

Pipe two layers of frosting on each layer of cake.

Pipe frosting ruffles over the whole cake.

Blueberry Cake
with Lemon Ganache

PROJECT COMPLEXITY:

YOU WILL NEED: *Blueberry cake (see page 32); Lemon ganache (see page 48); thawed frozen or fresh blueberries, to decorate*

CAKE PREPARATION TIME: 1 HOUR 35 MINUTES
LEMON GANACHE PREPARATION TIME: 1 HOUR 20 MINUTES
DECORATING TIME: 20 MINUTES

Cover the cake with lemon ganache.

Prepare the cake by filling and covering it with a thin layer of lemon ganache.

Fit a piping (icing) bag with a basket weave nozzle and spoon in the lemon ganache. Place the nozzle at the base of the cake with the smooth edge down and the ridge edge up. Pipe a straight ribbon vertically up the side of the cake. Pipe the next ribbon halfway overlapping the first one.

Continue to pipe until the whole cake is covered. With a palette knife smooth the top of the ribbons over the top of the cake.

Decorate the top with blueberries.

Overlap each piped ribbon slightly.

Vanilla Sponge Cake with Strawberry Ganache

PROJECT COMPLEXITY:

YOU WILL NEED: *Vanilla sponge cake (see page 18); Strawberry ganache (see page 48); Chocolate ganache (see page 46)*

CAKE PREPARATION TIME: 1 HOUR 50 MINUTES
STRAWBERRY GANACHE PREPARATION TIME: 1 HOUR 35 MINUTES
CHOCOLATE GANACHE PREPARATION TIME: 18 MINUTES
DECORATING TIME: 40 MINUTES

Cover the cake with strawberry ganache.

Pour warm chocolate ganache over the cake.

Prepare the cake by filling and covering it with the strawberry ganache.

Warm half of the chocolate ganache slightly in a bain-marie. Place the cake on a wire rack and pour the warm chocolate ganache over the top and side of the cake. Leave to set for 15 minutes.

Prepare a piping (icing) bag with a closed star nozzle and fill it with the remaining, slightly set, chocolate ganache. Pipe the whole top of the cake with roses and fill the gaps with stars.

chapter

7

COOKIE
DECORATIONS

DECORATING WITH Royal Icing

Royal icing can be used to create colourful decorations on top of cookies. Use a 'run out', as shown here, to maintain a clean outline.

1/// Fit a piping (icing) bag with a number 2 round nozzle and, using a medium stiff-peak royal icing, make a 'run out' by creating an outline offset slightly inside from the edge of the cookie.

2/// Fit another piping bag with a number 2 round nozzle and fill it with a softer, runny consistency of royal icing and flood the outlined shape to create a coloured section. If air bubbles appear on the surface, prick them with a cocktail stick or toothpick.

3/// Squeeze small drops of different colours to add more decoration.

To create the heart decoration shown above, pipe some dots and then drag a cocktail stick or toothpick through them.

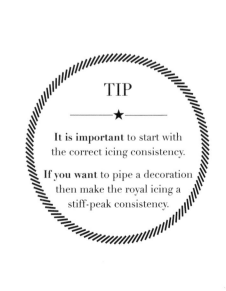

TIP

★

It is important to start with the correct icing consistency.

If you want to pipe a decoration then make the royal icing a stiff-peak consistency.

DECORATING WITH Sugarpaste

Creating your own cutters for use with sugarpaste (fondant) is great fun. The consistency of sugarpaste means it is very versatile, so extremely easy to use to decorate cookies.

1/// You can create your own bespoke cutters simply by drawing out the shapes of your choice on a piece of cardboard or heavy paper and then cutting around them with scissors.

2/// Roll out the sugarpaste (fondant) on a work surface lightly dusted with icing (confectioners') sugar to a thickness of 5 mm (¼ in). Place your chosen cutter on top and, with the point of a sharp knife, cut around the template.

3/// Lightly cover the bottom of the sugarpaste shape with edible glue and then carefully place it onto the cookie. Press down to secure it in position.

DECORATING WITH Stencils

Stencils can add that extra magical touch on top of iced cookies.
Choose a colourful glitter or dust for added effect.

1/// Roll out the sugarpaste (fondant) on a work surface lightly dusted with icing (confectioners') sugar to a thickness of 5 mm (¼ in). Place your chosen stencil on top.

2/// With your finger, coat the upperside of the stencil with a thin layer of shortening. Using a small paintbrush, apply the coloured dust or glitter liberally. Carefully remove the stencil.

3/// Cut out a shape using the same cutter you used for the cookies and carefully transfer it to the top of a cookie, securing it into position with edible glue.

STENCILS ARE A GREAT WAY TO ADD DETAILS QUICKLY.

★

BAKING SOS

Before we take a look at some specific problems that could occur, and how to overcome them, here are some very important general baking tips:

- Always read through the entire recipe before you start.
- Make sure you have all the ingredients ready and weighed out before beginning.
- Preheat the oven 15–20 minutes before you need it.
- Avoid overcrowding the cake tins in the oven because an even flow of heat is extremely important.

Now, let's tackle some of the most common problems:

BAKING

MY CAKE IS SINKING IN THE MIDDLE

There are many reasons why a cake sinks in the middle. It could be that you have over-beaten the mixture, that you have used an old baking powder, that the cake is not completely cooked (so test it towards the end of the baking time) or simply because you have opened the oven door too early and the sudden cool air has caused the cake to sink. Always try to wait at least 30 minutes before opening the oven door to check the cake.

MY CAKE IS BEGINNING TO BURN ON TOP BUT IS STILL UNCOOKED INSIDE

Make sure that the oven temperature isn't too high and place a piece of foil over the cake for the last 10–15 minutes.

CHOCOLATE CHIPS OR FRUITS ALWAYS SINK TO THE BOTTOM OF MY CAKES

Maybe you are making the mixture too loose.

A quick trick to overcome this problem is to coat the chocolate chips or fruits with a sprinkling of flour before adding to the mixture.

MY COOKIES ARE SPREADING OUT IN THE OVEN RATHER THAN KEEPING THEIR SHAPE

Make sure that when the recipe says 'cream the butter and sugar' you just mix them for 1 minute, or until well combined. Also, remember to chill the cookies before cooking and preheat the oven before using it.

CAKE DECORATING

I CAN'T GET MY EGG WHITES TO STIFFEN

There are a few reasons why egg whites will not stiffen. Perhaps you have over-whisked them, contaminated them with a bit of egg yolk or maybe the bowl wasn't pristinely clean to begin with.

MY BUTTERCREAM HAS CURDLED

Maybe the buttercream is too hot or you have added liquid to the mixture too fast. Increase the speed of the standmixer or place the bowl in the refrigerator to cool down and then begin the process of whisking again.

MY BUTTERCREAM PIPING IS MELTING

Place the bag of buttercream in the refrigerator for 5 minutes to help it firm up. Also, try to avoid overfilling the piping (icing) bag.

I CAN'T GET THE SUGARPASTE (FONDANT) LAYER SMOOTH

Perhaps the layer is too thin and, therefore, it is showing some of the imperfections on the surface of the cake. Make sure that the crumb coat you apply first is very smooth before you cover the cake with sugarpaste.

MY SUGARPASTE (FONDANT) HAS CRACKED

It could be that the sugarpaste has been rolled too thinly or because it is too old and dried out. Where possible, take the sugarpaste off and use a new piece or fill the crack with royal icing. Alternatively, you could wet some of the leftover sugarpaste to create a paste, smooth it over the top with your finger and remove the excess with some fabric.

THERE ARE AIR BUBBLES UNDER THE SUGARPASTE (FONDANT)

This will have been caused by air getting trapped under the sugarpaste. To remove air bubbles, simply prick the surface with a pin and gently press down to flatten the surface.

I CAN'T REMOVE THE SUGARPASTE (FONDANT) FROM ITS SILICONE MOULD

If the mould is deep or highly detailed and it's difficult to remove the paste, place the filled mould in the freezer for about 15 minutes so that the paste becomes firmer. It will then be easier to remove.

COOKIE DECORATING

MY COLOURS ARE BLEEDING

The term 'bleeding' refers to when one colour of icing is spreading into another one. The consistency of the icing is really important if you wish to avoid this. In order to check whether it is the right consistency or not, follow the '10-second rule': drag a palette knife through the surface of your icing and count to 10. If the surface becomes smooth somewhere between 5 and 10 seconds then the icing is ready; if it happens in less than 5 seconds, it is too runny (to rectify, mix it slowly, adding more icing/confectioners' sugar as you do so); if it takes more than 10 seconds, then the icing is too thick (to rectify this, mix it slowly, adding more water).

MY OUTLINE HAS DRIED UP AND BROKEN INTO LITTLE BITS

You may have over-beaten the royal icing. Remember to beat the icing only until it is glossy and just beginning to form a stiff peak.

MY FLOOD DECORATION BLEEDS INTO ONE COLOUR

Try to work on a batch of 5–6 biscuits at a time. First, do the flooding to all of them. Then, go back to the first one to add any other decorations like polka dots, stripes or any other design that requires a smooth pattern. This will ensure the first colour has had time to set.

MY DECORATION HAS A STREAKING EFFECT

This could be due to the fact that the icing is too runny or the water has separated from the icing (confectioners') sugar. To avoid this, make sure you mix the colour thoroughly and follow the '10-second rule' described above.

MY DECORATION COLOUR IS TOO DARK

When a colour dries it is usually a little deeper in colour than it was when first mixed up, so try to tint the icing a few hours before you need it, covering it with a clean damp cloth to prevent it from getting hard. And always make more than you need, as it is quite impossible to replicate the same colour.

Glossary

Bain-marie: also known as a water bath this is a technique used for cooking delicate food when a gentle and uniform heat is needed all around. Simply place a saucepan or a bowl above – but not touching – a larger saucepan of gently simmering water.

Baking paper: a heavy-duty grease- and moisture-resistant paper, widely used to line cake tins and cookie trays. It can also be used to make a paper piping (icing) bag.

Baking powder: a leavening agent containing bicarbonate of soda (baking soda) and cream of tartar that reacts when liquid is added to it.

Batter: this is the word used to refer to the uncooked mixture for cakes and cookies.

Bismarck nozzle: a type of nozzle specifically used to fill cupcakes (it is also called a piping tube nozzle).

Brown sugar: generally refers to fine, granulated sugar with a small amount of molasses. It is soft, sticky and tends to clump. Depending on the colour and flavour of the molasses used it is considered light or dark brown sugar.

Brush embroidery: a very popular decorating technique used to create a delicate lace effect. It refers to piped royal icing being brushed towards the centre of the design with a damp square-tipped paintbrush.

Buttermilk: the slightly sour liquid left after butter has been churned. Alternatively, you can sour the milk by adding some acid, such as lemon juice.

Chocolate modelling paste: also known as chocolate plastique. A versatile paste made with chocolate and glucose syrup. It is used to wrap cakes and make decorations such as flowers, ribbons and bows.

Cornelli lace: a popular decorating technique in which the lacy design depends on the continuous curving of icing strings that do not overlap or touch.

Crumb coat: this describes the small amount of buttercream that is spread out over a cake to prevent any cake crumbs from sticking to the final coating.

Edible dust colours: these are powdered colours that are generally used dry and dusted onto the surface of icing. They work very well with a stencil to create designs on top of iced cookies.

Flooding: when you fill the outlined area (*see* run out) with royal icing to create a smooth effect.

Ganache: a mixture that is made from chocolate and cream. It is used as a glaze, sauce or filling.

Glucose syrup: a clear, viscous, aqueous solution produced from the breakdown of starch. It is sold in jars or tubs in supermarkets. It can be used to soften texture, add volume, prevent crystallisation of sugar in processed foods (like jellies and jams) and enhance flavour.

Glycerine: a softening agent in the form of a clear and odourless syrup that has the property to attract moisture. It is used in cakes to help them stay moist.

Granulated sugar: this is the most common sweetener used in baking and is highly refined.

Icing (confectioners') sugar: consists of sucrose crystals finely pulverised into powder and available in various degrees of fineness.

Kneading: this process mixes ingredients and adds strength to the final product.

Lining a cake tin: when the inside of the cake tin is covered with baking paper in order to prevent the mixture from sticking to it.

Mascarpone: a fresh, thick, creamy Italian curd-style cheese made from cream, coagulated by the addition of citric acid. It has a very smooth texture with a milky and slightly sweet flavour.

Pearl (coarse) sugar: this has larger crystals than regular granulated sugar and can be coloured. This sugar makes a useful garnish on cupcakes or other baked goods.

Piping gel: a sweet gel that can be used in many different ways in cake decorating, such as glazing sugarpaste (fondant). It can also be added to buttercream to give elasticity if piping writing with it.

Polenta: cornmeal or maize flour made by grinding corn into flour. It has a rich yellow colour and a slightly sweet flavour.

Powdered gelatine: a colourless, tasteless, odourless setting agent that has been dried and broken up into individual grains.

Raw (demerara) sugar: a light brown sugar with large golden crystals. It can be used as a decorative coarse sugar.

Royal icing: a sweet, fluid paste made from whisked egg whites, icing (confectioners') sugar and lemon juice that sets solid.

Run out: making an outline shape of icing that will be flooded after. The key factor is to have a continuous border otherwise the flooding royal icing will flow out of it (*see* flooding).

Self-raising flour: plain (all-purpose) flour combined with a small amount of baking powder. You can make your own by adding 1 teaspoon of baking powder to every 110 g (3¾ oz/¾ cup) of plain flour.

Soft-ball stage: this describes a specific stage of heating sugar syrup to 118–120°C (244–248°F). Once it reaches this temperature, if you drop a bit of it into cold water to cool it down, it will form a soft ball. This method is used when making Italian meringue.

Soft peak: this is a term used to describe a consistency. For royal icing, it is when the icing is lifted from the bowl and the peak will not hold its shape. For whipped egg white, it refers to when peaks are formed – if the whisk is lifted the tip of the peaks will curl over.

Stiff peak: a term used to describe the consistency of royal icing or whipped egg white when it is stiff enough to hold a shape when lifted from the bowl.

Sugarpaste: a very sweet edible sugar dough used to cover cakes and make decorations. Also known as ready-to-roll fondant.

Sweeteners: can be divided into two main categories: dry crystalline sugars and syrups.

Torting: the technique used to divide a cake horizontally into more layers in order to add height as well as give a place to add fillings.

Vanilla bean: this is a sun-dried pod from a type of climbing orchid that has a soft, sweet flavour. It is long, black, thin and wrinkled and contains thousands of tiny black seeds, which can be extracted by opening the bean along its length and scraping out the inside using the tip of a small, sharp knife. If you cannot find a vanilla bean, substitute it with 1 teaspoon of natural vanilla extract.

Thanks...

I have enjoyed every single day that was spent creating this book – from the initial concept to the writing, tasting and final days of photography. But it couldn't have been done without the help of some incredible people …

Firstly, from the bottom of my heart, I would like to thank Catie Ziller for always supporting me and for being such an amazing friend – this book simply wouldn't have happened without you. An enormous thanks also to Deirdre Rooney for her stunning photographs, which made my creations so beautiful – we had so much fun together!

I would like to thank my publisher, Marabout, for giving me the opportunity to write this book.

A big thank you goes to Kathy Steer and Claire Musters for all their editorial work and to Alice Chadwick for her great design.

To my soul sisters, you know who you are, thanks for always supporting me.

To my children, Mario, Luca and Andrea, for being so patient and for understanding that all the cakes, cupcakes and cookies in the kitchen couldn't be eaten! To my husband, Salvatore, for giving me all the strength and support I could ever wish for and for always being available, even for those last-minute runs to buy more butter! Thank you.

A very special thank you goes to Brickett Davda for her beautiful plates, bowls and props and to The Olive Tree for their delicious food, which helped me and Deirdre get through the photo shoots.

SUPPLIERS

BAKER & MAKER
www.bakerandmaker.com

LAKELAND
www.lakeland.co.uk

BRICKETT DAVDA
www.brickettdavda.com

PIPII
www.pipii.co.uk

DIVERTIMENTI
www.divertimenti.co.uk

ROSE & GREY
www.roseandgrey.co.uk

ETSY
www.etsy.com

SQUIRES KITCHEN
www.squires-shop.com

HOBBY AND CRAFT
www.hobbycraft.co.uk

THE HAMBLEDON
www.thehambledon.com

JOHN LEWIS
www.johnlewis.com

BACKGROUNDS
www.backgroundsprophire.co.uk

Index

Published in 2016 by Murdoch Books, an imprint of Allen & Unwin
First published by Marabout (Hachette Livre) in 2014

Murdoch Books Australia
83 Alexander Street
Crows Nest NSW 2065
Phone: +61 (0) 2 8425 0100
Fax: +61 (0) 2 9906 2218
murdochbooks.com.au
info@murdochbooks.com.au

Murdoch Books UK
Ormond House
26-27 Boswell Street
London, WC1N 3JZ
Phone: +44 (0) 20 8785 5995
murdochbooks.co.uk
info@murdochbooks.co.uk

For Corporate Orders & Custom Publishing contact
Noel Hammond, National Business Development Manager, Murdoch Books Australia

Publisher: Corinne Roberts
Editors: Kathy Steer and Claire Musters
Design and illustration: Alice Chadwick
Photography: Deirdre Rooney
Translator: Melissa McMahon
Production Manager: Alexandra Gonzalez

A cataloguing-in-publication entry is available from the catalogue of the National Library
of Australia at nla.gov.au.

ISBN 978 1 74336 621 9 Australia
ISBN 978 1 74336 740 7 UK

A catalogue record for this book is available from the British Library.

Colour reproduction by Splitting Image Colour Studio Pty Ltd, Clayton, Victoria
Printed by 1010 Printing International Limited, China

IMPORTANT: Those who might be at risk from the effects of salmonella poisoning
(the elderly, pregnant women, young children and those suffering from immune deficiency
diseases) should consult their doctor with any concerns about eating raw eggs.

OVEN GUIDE: You may find cooking times vary depending on the oven you are using.
For fan-forced ovens, as a general rule, set the oven temperature to 20°C (35°F) lower than
indicated in the recipe.

MEASURES GUIDE: We have used 15 ml (3 teaspoon) tablespoon measures.